¡Bienvenido!

Just Enough **Spanish**

D. L. Ellis, R. Ellis

Pronunciation **Dr. J. Baldwin**

PASSPORT BOOKS
a division of *NTC Publishing Group*
Lincolnwood, Illinois USA

The publishers would like to thank the
Spanish National Tourist office for their help
during the preparation of this book

1992 Printing

This edition first published in 1983 by Passport Books,
a division of NTC Publishing Group,
4255 West Touhy Avenue,
Lincolnwood (Chicago), Illinois 60646-1975 U.S.A.
Originally published by Pan Books, © D.L. Ellis and R. Ellis,
1981. All rights reserved. No part of this book may be
reproduced, stored in a retrieval system, or transmitted in any
form, or by any means, electronic, mechanical, photocopying
or otherwise, without the prior permission of
NTC Publishing Group.
Manufactured in the United States of America.

2 3 4 5 6 7 8 9 0 AG 19 18 17 16 15 14 13 12 11

Contents

Using the phrase book

- This phrase book is designed to help you get by in Spanish-speaking countries, to get what you want or need. It concentrates on the simplest but most effective way you can express these needs in an unfamiliar language.
- The CONTENTS on p. 5 gives you a good idea of which section to consult for the phrase you need.
- The INDEX on p. 155 gives more detailed information about where to look for your phrase.
- When you have found the right page you will be given:

  either — the exact phrase

  or — help in making up a suitable sentence

  and — help to get the pronunciation right
- The English sentences in **bold type** will be useful for you in a variety of different situations, so they are worth learning by heart. (See also DO IT YOURSELF, p. 146.)
- Wherever possible you will find help in understanding what Spanish-speaking people say to *you*, in reply to your questions.
- If you want to practise the basic nuts and bolts of the language further, look at the DO IT YOURSELF section starting on p. 146.
- Note especially these three sections:

  Everyday expressions p. 11

  Shop talk p. 54

  Public notices p. 125

  You are sure to want to refer to them most frequently.
- When you arrive in a Spanish-speaking country, make good use of the tourist information offices (see p. 23)

US addresses:

Spanish National Tourist Office
665 Fifth Avenue
New York, NY 10022
(212) 759-8822

Venezuelan Consulate Office
7 East 51 Street
New York, NY 10022
(212) 826-1660

Mexican Government Tourist
  Office
405 Park Avenue
New York, NY 10022
(212) 755-7261

Argentine Consulate Office
12 W. 66th Street
New York, NY 10022
(212) 397-1400

A note on the pronunciation system

In traveler's phrase books there is usually a pronunciation section which tries to teach English-speaking tourists how to correctly pronounce the language of the country they are visiting. This is based on the belief that in order to be understood, the speaker must have an accurate, authentic accent—that he must pronounce every last word letter-perfectly.

The authors of this book, on the other hand, wanted to devise a workable and usable pronunciation system. So they had to face the fact it is absolutely impossible for an average speaker of English who has no technical training in phonetics and phonetic transcription systems (which includes 98% of all the users of this book!) to reproduce the sounds of a foreign language with perfect accuracy, just from reading a phonetic transcription, cold—no prior background in the language. We also believe that you don't have to have perfect pronunciation in order to make yourself understood in a foreign country. After all, natives you run into will take into account that you are foreigners, and visitors, and more than likely they will feel gratified by your efforts to communicate and will probably go out of their way to try to understand you. They may even help you, and correct you, in a friendly manner. We have found, also, that visitors to a foreign country are not usually concerned with perfect pronunciation—they just want to get their message across, to communicate!

With this in mind, we have designed a pronunciation system which is of the utmost simplicity to use. This system does not attempt to give an accurate—but also problematical and tedious—representation of the sound system of the language, but instead uses common sound and letter combinations in English which are the closest to the sounds in the foreign language. In this way, the sentences transcribed for pronunciation should be read as naturally as possible, as if they were ordinary English. In no way does the user have to attempt to make the words sound "foreign." So, while to yourselves you will sound as if you are speaking ordinary English—or at least making ordinary English sounds—you will at the same time be making yourselves understood in another language. And, as the saying goes, practice makes perfect, so it is probably a good idea to repeat aloud to yourselves several times the phrases you think you are going to use, before you actually use them. This will give you greater confidence, and will also help in making yourself understood.

In Spanish it is important to stress, or emphasize the syllables in italics, just as you would if we were to take as an English example: *Li*ttle Jack *Hor*ner *sat* in the *cor*ner. Here we have ten syllables but only four stresses.

Of course you may enjoy trying to pronounce a foreign language as well as possible and the present system is a good way to start. However, since it uses only the sounds of English, you will very soon need to depart from it as you imitate the sounds you hear the native speaker produce and begin to relate them to the spelling of the other language. Spanish will pose no problems as there is an obvious and consistent relationship between pronunciation and spelling.

¡Suerte!

Everyday expressions

[See also 'Shop Talk', p. 54]

Hello	**Hola**
	o-la
Good morning	**Buenos días**
	bwen-os dee*a*s
Good afternoon	**Buenas tardes**
	bwen-as t*a*rd-es
Goodnight	**Buenas noches**
	bwen-as n*o*ch-es
Good-bye	**Adiós**
	ad-y*o*s
See you later	**Hasta luego**
	*a*sta lweg-o
Yes	**Sí**
	see
Please	**Por favor**
	por fab-*o*r
Yes, please	**Sí, por favor**
	see por fab-*o*r
Great!	**¡Estupendo!**
	estoopendo
Thank you	**Gracias**
	gr*a*th-yas
Thank you very much	**Muchas gracias**
	m*o*ochas gr*a*th-yas
That's right	**Exacto**
	ex*a*cto
No	**No**
	no
No, thank you	**No, gracias**
	no gr*a*th-yas
I disagree	**No estoy de acuerdo**
	no est*o*y deh acw*a*ird*o*
Excuse me ⎤ Sorry ⎦	**Perdone**
	pairdon-eh
Don't mention it ⎤ That's OK ⎦	**De nada**
	deh n*a*-da

That's good I like it	**Está bien** esta bee-en
That's no good I don't like it	**No está bien** no esta bee-en
I know	**Ya sé** ya seh
I don't know	**No sé** no seh
It doesn't matter	**No importa** no importa
Where's the toilet, please?	**¿Dónde están los servicios, por favor?** dondeh estan los sairbith-yos por fab-or
How much is that? [*point*]	**¿Cuánto es?** cwanto es
Is the service included?	**¿Está incluido el servicio?** esta incloo-eedo el sairbith-yo
Do you speak English?	**¿Habla usted inglés?** abla oosted in-gles
I'm sorry ...	**Lo siento ...** lo see-ento ...
I don't speak Spanish	**no hablo español** no ablo espan-yol
I only speak a little Spanish	**sólo hablo un poco de español** sol-o ablo oon poco deh espan-yol
I don't understand	**no comprendo** no comprendo
Please can you ...	**Por favor, ¿puede ...** por fab-or pwed-eh ...
repeat that?	**repetir eso?** rep-eteer es-o
speak more slowly?	**hablar mas despacio?** ablar mas des-path-yo
write it down?	**escribirlo?** escrib-eerlo
What is this called in Spanish? [*point*]	**¿Cómo se llama esto en español?** com-o seh yama esto en espan-yol

Crossing the border

ESSENTIAL INFORMATION

- Don't waste time just before you leave rehearsing what you're going to say to the border officials – the chances are that you won't have to say anything at all, especially if you travel by air.
- It's more useful to check that you have your documents handy for the journey: passport, tickets, money, travellers' checks, insurance documents, driving licence and car registration documents.
- Look out for these signs:
  ADUANA   (customs)
  FRONTERA   (border)
  FUNCIONARIOS DE ADUANAS   (frontier police)
  CONTROL DE EQUIPAJES   (baggage control)
  [*For futher signs and notices, see p. 125*]
- You may be asked routine questions by the customs officials [*see below*]. If you have to give personal details see 'Meeting people', p. 14. The other important answer to know is 'Nothing': **Nada** (na-da)

ROUTINE QUESTIONS

Passport?	**¿Pasaporte?**
	pas-aporteh
Insurance?	**¿Seguro?**
	segoo-ro
Registration document? (logbook)	**¿Cartilla de propriedad?**
	cartee-ya deh prop-yed-ad
Ticket, please	**Billete, por favor**
	bee-yet-eh por fab-or
Have you anything to declare?	**¿Tiene algo que declarar?**
	tee-en-eh algo keh decla-rar
Where are you going?	**¿A dónde va usted?**
	ah dondeh ba oosted
How long are you staying?	**¿Cuánto tiempo va a quedarse?**
	cwanto tee-empo ba ah ked-ar-seh
Where have you come from?	**¿De dónde viene usted?**
	deh dondeh bee-eneh oosted

You may also have to fill in forms which ask for:

surname	**apellido**
first name	**nombre**
maiden name	**nombre de soltera**
place of birth	**lugar de nacimiento**
date of birth	**fecha de nacimiento**
address	**dirección**
nationality	**nacionalidad**
profession	**profesión**
passport number	**número de pasaporte**
issued at	**expedido en**
signature	**firma**

Meeting people

[*See also 'Everyday expressions', p. 11*]

Breaking the ice

Hello	**Hola**
	o-la
Good morning	**Buenos días**
	bwen-os d*ee*as
How are you?	**¿Cómo está usted?**
	com-o est*a* oost*e*d
Pleased to meet you	**Mucho gusto**
	m*oo*cho g*oo*sto
I am here ...	**Estoy aquí ...**
	estoy ak-*ee* ...
on holiday	**de vacaciones**
	deh bakath-y*on*-es
on business	**de negocios**
	deh negoth-yos
Can I offer you ...	**¿Puedo ofrecerle ...**
	pwed-o ofreth*air*-leh ...
a drink?	**una bebida?**
	*oo*na beb-*ee*da

a cigarette?

un cigarrillo?
oon thiggar*ee*-yo

a cigar?

un puro?
oon p*oo*-ro

Are you staying long?

¿Va a quedarse mucho tiempo?
b*a* ah ked-*a*r-seh m*oo*cho tee-*e*mpo

Name

What is your name?

¿Cómo se llama?
com-o seh *y*ama

My name is ...

Me llamo ...
meh *y*amo ...

Family

Are you married?

¿Es usted casado/a?*
*e*s oosted cas*a*d-o/-ah

I am ...

Soy ...
s*o*y ...

married

casado/a*
cas*a*d-o/-ah

single

soltero/a*
solt*ai*ro/-ah

This is ...

Le presento a ...
leh pres-*e*nto ah

my wife

mi esposa
mee esp*o*s-ah

my husband

mi marido
mee ma-r*ee*do

my son

mi hijo
mee *ee*ho

my daughter

mi hija
mee *ee*ha

my (boy) friend

mi novio
mee n*o*b-yo

my (girl) friend

mi novia
mee n*o*b-ya

my (male/female) colleague

mi colega
mee col-*e*g-ah

Do you have any children?

¿Tiene hijos?
tee-*e*n-eh *ee*ho*s*

*For men use 'o', for women 'a'

I have ...	**Tengo ...**
	tengo ...
one daughter	**una hija**
	*oo*na *ee*ha
one son	**un hijo**
	oon *ee*ho
two daughters	**dos hijas**
	dos *ee*has
three sons	**tres hijos**
	tres *ee*hos
No, I haven't any children	**No, no tengo hijos**
	no no tengo *ee*hos

Where you live

Are you ...	**¿Es usted ...**
	es oosted ...
Spanish?	**español/a?**
	espan-y*o*l/ah
South American?	**sudamericano/a?**
	sooda*me*ric*a*no/ah
I am ...	**Soy ...**
	soy ...
American	**americano/a**
	ameri*ca*no/ah
English	**inglés/a**
	in-gles/ah

[For other nationalities, see p. 138]

Where are you from?

I live ...	**Vivo ...**
	bee-bo ...
in London	**en Londres**
	en *lo*ndres
in England	**en Inglaterra**
	en ingla-*te*rra
in the north	**en el norte**
	en el *no*rteh
in the south	**en el sur**
	en el *soo*r
in the east	**en el este**
	en el *e*steh

in the west	**en el oeste**
	en el o-*esteh*
in the centre	**en el centro**
	en el *thentro*

[*For other countries, see p. 138*]

For the businessman and woman

I'm from ... (firm's name)	**Soy de ...**
	soy deh ...
I have an appointment with ...	**Tengo una cita con ...**
	tengo *oo*na *theet*a con ...
May I speak to ... ?	**¿Puedo hablar con ... ?**
	pwed-o abl*ar* con ...
This is my card	**Esta es mi tarjeta**
	esta es mee tar-*het*-ah
I'm sorry I'm late	**Siento llegar tarde**
	see-ento yeg-*ar* *tardeh*
Can I fix another appointment?	**¿Puedo fijar otra cita?**
	pwed-o fee-h*ar* *ot*-ra th*eet*a
I'm staying at the hotel (Madrid)	**Estoy en el hotel (Madrid)**
	est*oy* en el ot-*el* (madr*id*)
I'm staying in (St John's) road	**Estoy en la calle (San Juan)**
	est*oy* en la c*a*-yeh (san hwan)

Asking the way

ESSENTIAL INFORMATION

- Keep a look out for all these place names as you will find them on shops, maps and notices.

WHAT TO SAY

Excuse me, please	**Perdone, por favor**
	pairdon-eh por fab-*or*

How do I get ...
¿**Para ir ...**
para eer ...

to Madrid?
a Madrid?
ah madreed

to calle Alfonso Primero?
a la calle Alfonso Primero?
ah la ca-yeh alfonso prim-airo

to the Hotel Castilla?
al hotel Castilla?
al ot-el castee-ya

to the airport?
al aeropuerto?
al airo-pwairto

to the beach?
a la playa?
ah la pla-ya

to the bus station?
a la estación de autobuses?
ah la estath-yon deh ah-ooto-booses

to the historic site?
a la ciudad antigua?
ah la thee-oodad antigwa

to the market?
al mercado?
al maircad-o

to the police station?
a la comisaría de policía?
ah la comisareea deh politheea

to the port?
al puerto?
al pwairto

to the post office?
a correos?
ah cor-reh-os

to the railway station?
a la estación de tren?
ah la estath-yon deh tren

to the sports stadium?
al estadio de deportes?
al estad-yo deh dep-ort-es

to the tourist information office?
a la oficina de información y turismo?
ah la ofitheena deh informath-yon ee too-rismo

to the town centre?
al centro de la ciudad?
al thentro deh la thee-oodad

to the town hall?
al ayuntamiento?
al a-yoontam-yento

Excuse me, please
Perdone, por favor
pairdon-eh por fab-or

Is there ... near by?
¿**Hay ... cerca?**
ah-ee ... thairca

an art gallery
una galería de arte
oona gal-ereea deh arteh

a baker's	una panadería
	oona panad-ereeah
a bank	un banco
	oon banco
a bar	un bar
	oon bar
a botanical garden	un jardín botánico
	oon hardeen botanic-o
a bus stop	una parada de autobús
	oona parad-ah deh ah-ooto-boos
a butcher's	una carnicería
	oona carnith-ereea
a café	una cafetería
	oona cafet-ereea
a cake shop	una pastelería
	oona pastel-ereea
a campsite	un camping
	oon camping
a car park	un aparcamiento
	oon aparcam-yento
a change bureau	una oficina de cambio
	oona ofitheena deh camb-yo
a chemist's	una farmacia
	oona farmath-ya
a church	una iglesia
	oona eegles-ya
a cinema	un cine
	oon thin-eh
a delicatessen	una mantequería
	oona mantek-ereea
a dentist's	un dentista
	oon dentista
a department store	unos almacenes
	oonos almath-en-es
a disco	una discoteca
	oona discotec-ah
a doctor's surgery	un consultorio médico
	oon consooltorio medic-o
a dry cleaner's	una tintorería
	oona tintor-ereea
a fishmonger's	una pescadería
	oona pescad-ereea

Is there . . . near by?　　　　¿Hay . . . cerca?
　　　　　　　　　　　　　　　ah-ee . . . thairca

　　a garage (for repairs)　　un garaje
　　　　　　　　　　　　　　　oon ga-*rah*eh

　　a greengrocer's　　una verdulería
　　　　　　　　　　　　　　　*oo*na berdool-er*ee*a

　　a grocer's　　una tienda de comestibles
　　　　　　　　　　　　　　　oona tee-enda deh com-est*ee*-bles

　　a hairdresser's　　una peluquería
　　　　　　　　　　　　　　　*oo*na pelook-er*ee*a

　　a hardware shop　　una ferretería
　　　　　　　　　　　　　　　*oo*na ferret-er*ee*a

　　a Health and Social　　una oficina de la Seguridad
　　　Security Office　　　Social
　　　　　　　　　　　　　　　*oo*na ofith*ee*na deh la
　　　　　　　　　　　　　　　segoo-reed*ad* soth-y*al*

　　a hospital　　un hospital
　　　　　　　　　　　　　　　oon ospit*al*

　　a hotel　　un hotel
　　　　　　　　　　　　　　　oon ot-*el*

　　an ice-cream parlour　　una heladería
　　　　　　　　　　　　　　　*oo*na ellad-er*ee*a

　　a laundry　　una lavandería
　　　　　　　　　　　　　　　*oo*na laband-er*ee*a

　　a museum　　un museo
　　　　　　　　　　　　　　　oon moo-s*ey*-o

　　a newsagent's　　una tienda de periódicos
　　　　　　　　　　　　　　　*oo*na tee-enda deh peri-*o*dicos

　　a nightclub　　una sala de fiestas
　　　　　　　　　　　　　　　*oo*na sal-ah deh fee-*es*tas

　　a park　　un parque
　　　　　　　　　　　　　　　oon p*ar*keh

　　a petrol station　　una gasolinera
　　　　　　　　　　　　　　　*oo*na gasolin-*er*ra

　　a post box　　un buzón
　　　　　　　　　　　　　　　oon booth*on*

　　a public garden　　un jardín público
　　　　　　　　　　　　　　　oon hard*een* p*oo*blico

　　a public toilet　　unos servicios públicos
　　　　　　　　　　　　　　　*oo*nos sairb*ith*-yos p*oo*blicos

　　a restaurant　　un restaurante
　　　　　　　　　　　　　　　oon resta-oor*an*teh

a snack bar	**un bar**
	oon b*a*r
a sports ground	**un campo de deportes**
	oon c*a*mpo deh dep-*o*rt-es
a supermarket	**un supermercado**
	oon supermairc*a*d-o
a sweet shop	**una bombonería**
	*oo*na bombon-er*ee*a
a swimming pool	**una piscina**
	oona pis-th*ee*na
a taxi stand	**una parada de taxis**
	*oo*na par*a*d-ah deh t*a*xis
a telephone	**un teléfono**
	oon tel*e*f-ono
a theatre	**un teatro**
	oon teh-*a*tro
a tobacconist's	**un estanco**
	oon est*a*nco
a travel agent's	**una agencia de viajes**
	*oo*na ahenth-ya deh bee-*ah*-hes
a youth hostel	**un albergue juvenil**
	oon alb*a*ir-geh hooben-*ee*l
a zoo	**un zoo**
	oon th*oh*-o

DIRECTIONS

- Asking where a place is, or if a place is near by, is one thing; making sense of the answer is another.
- Here are some of the most important key directions and replies.

Left	**Izquierda**
	ithk-*yair*da
Right	**Derecha**
	der*e*ch-ah
Straight on	**Todo recto**
	t*o*do r*e*cto
There	**Allí**
	ay*ee*

First left/right	**La primera a la izquierda/derecha**
	la prim-*air*a ah la ithk-y*air*da/
	der*ech*-a
Second left/right	**La segunda a la izquiera/derecha**
	la seg-*oo*nda ah la ithk-y*air*da/
	der*ech*-a
At the crossroads	**En el cruce**
	en el cr*oo*theh
At the traffic lights	**En el semáforo**
	en el sem*a*foro
At the roundabout	**En el cruce giratorio**
	en el cr*oo*theh gee-rator*ee*-o
At the level crossing	**En el paso a nivel**
	en el p*as*-o ah nib-*el*
It's near/far	**Está cerca/lejos**
	esta th*air*ca/l*eh*-hos
One kilometre	**A un kilómetro**
	ah oon kil*o*metro
Two kilometres	**A dos kilómetros**
	ah dos kil*o*metros
Five minutes ...	**A cinco minutos ...**
	ah th*in*-co min*oo*tos ...
on foot	**a pie**
	a pee-*eh*
by car	**en coche**
	en *coch*-eh
Take ...	**Tome ...**
	t*om*-eh ...
the bus	**el autobús**
	el ah-ooto-b*oo*s
the train	**el tren**
	el tr*en*
the tram	**el tranvía**
	el tramb*ee*a
the underground	**el metro**
	el m*e*tro

[*For public transport, see p. 116*]

The tourist information office

ESSENTIAL INFORMATION

- Most towns and even some villages in Spanish-speaking countries have a tourist information office.
- Look for these words:
  OFICINA DE INFORMACION Y TURISMO
  DELEGACION PROVINCIAL DE INFORMACION Y TURISMO
  OFICINA MUNICIPAL DE INFORMACION
- Sometimes there may be signposts with these abbreviations: **MIT (Ministerio de Información y Turismo)** and **CITE (Centro de Iniciativas Turísticas Españolas).**
- These offices provide free information in the form of printed leaflets, fold-outs, brochures, lists and plans.
- You may have to pay for some types of document but this is not usual.
- For finding a tourist office, see p. 17.

WHAT TO SAY

Please, have you got ...	**Por favor, ¿tiene ...**
	por fa-bor tee-en-eh ...
a plan of the town?	**un plano de la ciudad?**
	oon plan-o deh la thee-oodad
a list of hotels?	**una lista de hoteles?**
	oona leesta deh ot-el-es
a list of campsites?	**una lista de campings?**
	oona leesta de campings
a list of restaurants	**una lista de restaurantes?**
	oona leesta deh resta-oorant-es
a list of coach excursions?	**una lista de excursiones en autobús?**
	oona leesta deh excoors-yon-es en ah-ooto-boos
a leaflet on the town?	**un folleto de la ciudad?**
	oon foyeto deh la thee-oodad
a leaflet on the region?	**un folleto de la región?**
	oon foyeto deh la reh-hee-on

Please, have you got ...	**Por favor, ¿tiene ...**
	por fa-bor tee-en-eh ...
a railway timetable?	**un horario de trenes?**
	oon orarrio deh tren-es
a bus timetable?	**un horario de autobuses?**
	oon orarrio deh ah-ooto-boos-es
In English, please	**En inglés, por favor**
	en in-gles por fab-or
How much do I owe you?	**¿Cuánto le debo?**
	cwanto leh deb-o
Can you recommend ...	**¿Puede recomendarme ...**
	pwed-eh recommendar-meh ...
a cheap hotel?	**un hotel barato?**
	oon ot-el ba-rat-o
a cheap restaurant?	**un restaurante barato?**
	oon resta-ooranteh ba-rat-o
Can you make a booking for me?	**¿Puede hacerme una reserva?**
	pwed-eh athair-meh oona res-airba

LIKELY ANSWERS

You need to understand when the answer is 'No'. You should be able to tell by the assistant's facial expression, tone of voice and gesture, but there are some language clues, such as:

No	**No**
	no
I'm sorry	**Lo siento**
	lo see-ento
I don't have a list of campsites	**No tengo una lista de campings**
	no tengo oona leesta deh campings
I haven't got any left	**No me queda ninguno**
	no meh ked-ah nin-goono
It's free	**Es gratis**
	es grat-is

Accommodation

Hotel

ESSENTIAL INFORMATION

- If you want hotel-type accommodation, all the following words in capital letters are worth looking for on name boards:
  HOTEL (accommodation with all facilities, the quality depending on the star rating)
  HOTEL-RESIDENCIA (similar to the above but often for longer stays)
  PENSION (small, privately run hotel)
  HOSTAL
  FONDA (a modest form of pensión)
  MOTEL
  ALBERGUE (often picturesque type of hotel situated in the countryside)
  PARADOR (converted palaces and castles in recognized beauty spots – relatively expensive)
- The last two are run by the **Secretaria de Estado de Turismo** (Secretary of State for Tourism).
- In some places, you will find the following: **CAMAS** (beds), **HABITACIONES** (rooms), **CASA** (house) followed by the owner's name or **CASA DE HUESPEDES** (guest house) – these are all alternatives to a pensión.
- Hotels are divided into five classes (from luxury to tourist class and **pensiones** into three.
- A list of hotels and **pensiones** in the town or district can usually be obtained at the local tourist information office [see p. 23]
- The cost is displayed in the room itself, so you can check it when having a look around before agreeing to stay.
- The displayed cost is for the room itself, per night and not per person. Breakfast is extra and therefore optional.
- Service and VAT is always included in the cost of the room, so tipping is voluntary. In Spain, however, it is normal practice to tip porters and waiters.

- Not all hotels provide meals, apart from breakfast. **A pensión** always provides meals. Breakfast is continental style: coffee/tea with rolls and jam.
- When registering you will be asked to leave your passport at the reception desk and to complete a form.
- Finding a hotel, see p. 17.

WHAT TO SAY

I have a booking	**Tengo una reserva**
	*te*ngo *oo*na res-*air*ba
Have you any vacancies, please?	**¿Tiene habitaciones libres, por favor?**
	tee-*en*-eh abeetath-yon-es
	lee-bres por fab-*or*
Can I book a room?	**¿Puedo reservar una habitación?**
	p*wed*-o res-air*bar oo*na abeetath-yon
It's for ...	**Es para ...**
	es para ...
one person	**una persona**
	*oo*na pairson-ah
two people	**dos personas**
	d*os* pairson-as

[For numbers, see p. 131]

It's for ...	**Es para ...**
	es para ...
one night	**una noche**
	*oo*na noch-eh
two nights	**dos noches**
	d*os* noch-es
one week	**una semana**
	*oo*na sem-*a*nna
two weeks	**dos semanas**
	d*os* sem-*a*nnas
I would like ...	**Quiero ...**
	kee-*airo* ...
a (quiet) room	**una habitación (tranquila)**
	*oo*na abeetath-yon (trank*ee*-ya)

two rooms	**dos habitaciones**
	dos abeetath-yon-es
with a single bed	**con una cama individual**
	con oona cam-ah indibid-wal
with two single beds	**con dos camas individuales**
	con dos cam-as indibid-wal-es
with a double bed	**con una cama doble**
	con oona cam-ah dobleh
with a toilet	**con servicio**
	con sairbith-yo
with a bathroom	**con baño**
	con ban-yo
with a shower	**con ducha**
	con doocha
with a cot	**con una cuna**
	con oona coona
with a balcony	**con balcón**
	con balcon
I would like ...	**Quiero ...**
	kee-airo ...
full board	**pensión completa**
	pens-yon complet-ah
half board	**media pensión**
	med-ya pens-yon
bed and breakfast	**desayuno incluido**
	desa-yoono incloo-eedo
[*See Essential information*]	
Do you serve meals?	**¿Sirven comidas?**
	seerben com-eedas
At what time is ...	**¿A qué hora es ...**
	ah keh ora es ...
breakfast?	**el desayuno?**
	el desa-yoono
lunch?	**la comida?**
	la com-eeda
dinner?	**la cena?**
	la then-ah
How much is it?	**¿Cuánto es?**
	cwanto es
Can I look at the room?	**¿Puedo ver la habitación?**
	pwed-o bair la abeetath-yon

I'd prefer a room ...
Prefiero una habitación ...
pref-*yair*-o *oo*na abeetath-*y*on ...

at the front/at the back
exterior/interior
exterri-*or*/ interri-*or*

OK, I'll take it
Está bien, la tomo
est*a* bee-en la tom-o

No thanks, I won't take it
No gracias, no la tomo
no grath-yas no la tom-o

The key to number (10), please
La llave de la número (diez), por favor
la y*ab*-eh deh la noomairo (dee-*e*th) por fab-*or*

Please, may I have ...
Por favor, ¿puede darme ...
por fab-*or* pwed-eh d*ar*meh ...

a coat hanger?
una percha?
*oo*na p*air*cha

a towel?
una toalla?
*oo*na toh-*al*-ya

a glass?
un vaso?
*oo*n b*ass*o

some soap?
jabón?
hab-*on*

an ashtray?
un cenicero?
*oo*n thenee-th*air*-o

another pillow?
otra almohada?
ot-ra almo-*ad*-ah

another blanket?
otra manta?
ot-ra m*a*nta

Come in!
¡Adelante!
ad-el-*a*nteh

One moment, please!
¡Un momento, por favor!
*oo*n momento por fab-*or*

Please can you ...
Por favor, ¿puede ...
por fab-*or* pwed-eh ...

do this laundry/dry cleaning?
lavar esto/limpiar esto en seco?
lab-*ar* esto/limp-y*ar* esto en sec-o

call me at ... ?
llamarme a ... ?
ya-m*ar*meh ah ...

help me with my luggage?
ayudarme con el equipaje?
a-yood*ar*meh con el ekeep*a*-heh

call me a taxi for ... ?
llamarme un taxi para ... ?
ya-m*ar*meh *oo*n t*a*xi p*a*ra ...

[For times, see p. 133]

The bill, please	**La cuenta, por favor**
	la cwenta por fab-or
Is service included?	**¿Está incluido el servicio?**
	esta incloo-eedo el sairbith-yo
I think this is wrong	**Creo que esto está mal**
	creh-o keh esto esta mal
Can you give me a receipt?	**¿Puede darme un recibo?**
	pwed-eh darmeh oon retheebo

At breakfast

Some more . . . , please	**Mas . . . , por favor**
	mas . . . por fab-or
coffee	**café**
	cafeh
tea	**té**
	teh
bread	**pan**
	pan
butter	mantequilla
	mantehkee-ya
jam	mermelada
	mairmel-ad-ah
May I have a boiled egg?	**¿Puedo haber un huevo pasado**
	por agua?
	pwed-o abair oon web-o
	pasad-o por agwa

LIKELY REACTIONS

Have you an identity document, please?	**¿Tiene usted un documento de identidad, por favor?**
	tee-en-eh oosted oon docoomento deh id-entidad por fab-or
What's your name? [see p. 14]	**¿Cómo se llama?**
	com-o seh yama
Sorry, we're full	**Lo siento, está lleno**
	lo see-ento esta yen-o
I haven't any rooms left	**No me quedan habitaciones**
	no meh ked-an abeetath-yon-es
Do you want to have a look?	**¿Quiere ver la habitación?**
	kee-aireh bair la abeetath-yon

How many people is it for?	**¿Para cuántas personas es?**
	para cwantas pairson-as es
From (seven o'clock) onwards	**Desde (las siete) en adelante**
	desdeh (las see-et-eh) en
	ad-el-anteh
From (midday) onwards	**Desde (mediodía) en adelante**
	desdeh (med-yo deea) en
	ad-el-anteh
[For times, see p. 133]	
It's (1000) pesetas	**Son (mil) pesetas**
[For numbers, see p. 131]	son (mil) pes-et-as

Camping and youth hostelling

ESSENTIAL INFORMATION

Camping
- Look for the word: **CAMPING**
- Be prepared to have to pay:
  per person
  for the car (if applicable)
  for the tent or caravan plot
  for electricity
  for hot showers
- You must provide proof of identity such as your passport.
- In Spain, most campsites are situated along the coast and those inland are few and far between. You can camp off-site with the permission of the authorities and/or the landowner; however, there are a number of regulations governing where you can or cannot camp—the Spanish Tourist Office in New York has details so check with them before travelling abroad.
- Camping carnets are no longer essential but advisable as they do provide third-party insurance for those camping off-site.
- During the high season it is advisable to book in advance by writing direct to the campsite.
- Persons under the age of sixteen are not admitted on a site unless accompanied by an adult.

Youth hostels

- Look for the words: **ALBERGUE JUVENIL.**
- You will be asked for a YHA card and passport on arrival.
- Food and cooking facilities vary from hostel to hostel and you may have to help with the domestic chores.
- You must take your own sleeping bag lining but bedding can sometimes be hired on arrival.
- In the high season it is advisable to book beds in advance, and your stay will be limited to a maximum of three consecutive nights per hostel.
- Apply to the Spanish Tourist office in New York or local tourist offices in Spain [*see p. 23*] for lists of youth hostels and details of regulations for hostellers.
- For buying or replacing camping equipment, see p. 52.

WHAT TO SAY

I have a booking	**Tengo una reserva** tengo *oo*na res-*air*ba
Have you any vacancies?	**¿Tiene plazas libres?** tee-en-eh plathas *lee*-bres
It's for ...	**Es para ...** es para ...
one adult/one person	**un adulto/una persona** oon ad*oo*lto/*oo*na pairson-ah
two adults/two people	**dos adultos/dos personas** dos ad*oo*ltos/dos pairson-as
and one child	**y un niño** ee oon neen-yo
and two children	**y dos niños** ee dos neen-yos
It's for ...	**Es para ...** es para ...
one night	**una noche** *oo*na noch-eh
two nights	**dos noches** dos noch-es
one week	**una semana** *oo*na sem-*a*nna
two weeks	**dos semanas** dos sem-*a*nnas

How much is it ...	**¿Cuánto es ...**
	cwanto es ...
for the tent?	**por la tienda?**
	por la tee-enda
for the caravan?	**por la caravana?**
	por la caraban-ah
for the car?	**por el coche?**
	por el coch-eh
for the electricity?	**por la electricidad**
	por la electrithee-dad
per person?	**por persona?**
	por pairson-ah
per day/night?	**por día/noche?**
	por deea/noch-eh
May I look round?	**¿Puedo mirar?**
	pwed-o mee-rar
Do you close the gate/door at night?	**¿Cierran la puerta por la noche?**
	thee-erran la pwairta por la noch-eh
Do you provide anything ...	**¿Dan ustedes algo ...**
	dan oosted-es algo ...
to eat?	**de comer?**
	deh com-air
to drink?	**de beber?**
	deh beb-air
Is there/are there ...	**¿Hay ...**
	ah-ee ...
a bar?	**bar?**
	bar
hot showers?	**duchas calientes?**
	doochas cal-yentes
a kitchen?	**cocina?**
	cotheena
a laundry?	**lavandería?**
	laband-ereea
a restaurant?	**restaurante?**
	resta-ooranteh
a shop?	**tienda?**
	tee-enda
a swimming pool?	**piscina?**
	pis-theena

a takeaway?
[*For food shopping, see p. 59, and for eating and drinking out, see p. 80*]

tienda de comidas preparadas?
tee-enda deh com-*ee*das
   prepa-rad-as

I would like a counter for the shower

Quiero una ficha para la ducha
kee-*airo* *oo*na f*ee*cha para la
   d*oo*cha

Where are . . .

¿Dónde están . . .
dondeh estan . . .

the dustbins?

los cubos de basura?
los c*oo*bos deh bas*oo*-ra

the showers?

las duchas?
las d*oo*chas

the toilets?

los servicios?
los sairb*i*th-yos

At what time must one . . .

¿A qué hora debe uno . . .
ah keh *o*ra deb-eh *oo*no . . .

go to bed?

acostarse?
acost*ar*-seh

get up?

levantarse?
leb-ant*ar*-seh

Please, have you got . . .

Por favor, ¿tiene . . .
por fab-or tee-en-eh . . .

a broom?

una escoba?
*oo*na escob-ah

a corkscrew?

un sacacorchos?
*oo*n sac-ac*or*chos

a drying-up cloth?

un paño de cocina?
*oo*n pan-yo deh cot*heena*

a fork?

un tenedor?
*oo*n ten-ed-*o*r

a fridge?

un frigorífico?
*oo*n frig-or*i*fico

a frying pan?

una sartén?
*oo*na sart*en*

an iron?

una plancha?
*oo*na pl*a*ncha

a knife?

un cuchillo?
*oo*n cooch*ee*-yo

a plate?

un plato?
*oo*n pl*a*t-o

Please, have you got ...	Por favor, ¿tiene ... por fab-*or* tee-*en*-eh ...
a saucepan?	**una cacerola?** *oo*na cathth-r*ol*-ah
a teaspoon?	**una cucharilla?** *oo*na coochar*ee*-ya
a tin opener?	**un abrelatas?** *oo*n abrel-*at*-as
any washing powder?	**detergente?** det-air-h*en*teh
any washing-up liquid?	**lavavajillas?** lababa-h*ee*-yas
The bill, please	**La cuenta, por favor** la c*wen*ta por fab-*or*

Problems

The toilet	**El servicio** el sairb*ith*-yo
The shower	**La ducha** la d*oo*cha
The tap	**El grifo** el gr*ee*fo
The razor point	**El enchufe de la maquinilla de afeitar** el ench*oo*feh deh la makin*ee*-ya deh affaytar
The light	**La luz** la l*oo*th
... is not working	**... está roto/a** ... est*a* r*o*t-o/ah
My camping gas has run out	**Mi camping gas se ha acabado** mee c*a*mping g*a*s seh *a*h acab*a*d-o

LIKELY REACTIONS

Have you an identity
  document?

¿Tiene usted un documento de
  identidad?
tee-en-eh oosted oon docoomento
  deh id-entidad

Your membership card,
  please

Su carnet, por favor
soo carnet por fab-or

What's your name? *[see p. 14]* ¿Cómo se llama?
com-o seh yama

Sorry, we're full

Lo siento, está lleno
lo see-ento esta yen-o

How many people is it for?

¿Para cuántas personas es?
para cwantas pairson-as es

How many nights is it for?

¿Para cuántas noches es?
para cwantas noch-es es

It's (100) pesetas . . .

Son (cien) pesetas . . .
son (thee-en) pes-et-as . . .

  per day/per night

por día/por noche
por deea/por noch-eh

[For numbers, see p. 131]

Rented accommodation: problem solving

ESSENTIAL INFORMATION

- If you're looking for accommodation to rent, look out for:
  SE ALQUILA (for rent)
  PISO (flat)
  APARTAMENTO (apartment)
  VILLA (villa)
  CHALET (chalet)
  CASA DE CAMPO (cottage)
  FINCA (country house)
- For arranging details of your let, see 'Hotel' p. 25.
- Key words you will meet if renting on the spot:
  la finanza (deposit)   **la llave** (key)
  la fee-*a*ntha   la y*a*b-eh
- Having arranged your own accommodation and arrived with the key,
  check the obvious basics that you take for granted at home.
  Electricity Voltage? Razors and small appliances brought from home
  may need adjusting. You may need an adaptor.
  Gas Town gas or bottled gas? Butane gas must be kept indoors,
  propane gas must be kept outdoors.
  Stove Don't be surprised to find:
  the grill inside the oven, or no grill at all
  a lid covering the rings which lifts up to form a 'splash-back'
  a mixture of two gas rings and two electric rings.
  Toilet Mains drainage or septic tank? Don't flush disposable diapers
  or anything else down the toilet if you are on a septic tank.
  Water Find the stopcock. Check taps and plugs — they may not
  operate in the way you are used to. Check how to turn on (or light)
  the hot water.
  Windows Check the method of opening and closing windows and
  shutters.
  Insects Is an insecticide spray provided? If not, get one locally.
  Equipment For buying or replacing equipment, see p. 52.
- You will probably have an official agent, but be clear in your own
  mind who to contact in an emergency, even if it is only a neighbour
  in the first instance.

WHAT TO SAY

My name is ...	Me llamo ... meh yam-o ...
I'm staying at ...	Estoy en ... estoy en ...
They've cut off ..	Han cortado ... an cortad-o ...
the electricity	la electricidad la electrithee-dad
the gas	el gas el gas
the water	el agua el agwa
Is there ... in the area?	¿Hay ... en el área? ah-ee ... en el a-reh-a
an electrician	un electricista oon electri-thista
a plumber	un fontanero oon fontan-airo
a gas fitter	un empleado del gas oon empleh-ad-o del gas
Where is ...	¿Dónde está ... dondeh esta ...
the fuse box?	la caja de fusibles la ca-ha deh foosee-bles
the stopcock?	la llave de paso? la yab-eh deh pas-o
the boiler?	la caldera? la caldaira
the water heater?	el calentador del agua? el callenta-dor del agwa
Is there ...	¿Hay ... ah-ee ...
town gas?	gas ciudad? gas thee-oodad
bottled gas?	gas en botella? gas en botel-ya
a septic tank?	cisterna? thistairna
central heating?	calefacción central? callefak-thion thentral

The cooker	**La cocina**
	la coth*ee*na
The hair dryer	**El secador**
	el sec-a-d*o*r
The heating	**La calefacción**
	la callefak-thi*o*n
The immersion heater	**El calentador de immersión**
	el callenta-d*o*r deh inmairs-y*o*n
The iron	**La plancha**
	la pl*a*ncha
The pilot light	**La luz del piloto**
	la l*oo*th del pil-*o*t-o
The refrigerator	**El frigorífico**
	el frig-or*i*fico
The telephone	**El teléfono**
	el tel*e*f-ono
The toilet	**El servicio**
	el sairb*i*th-yo
The washing machine	**La lavadora**
	la lab-a-d*o*ra
... is not working	**... está roto/a**
	... est*a* r*o*t-o/-ah
Where can I get ...	**¿Dónde puedo obtener ...**
	d*o*ndeh pw*e*d-o obten-*air* ...
an adaptor for this?	**un adaptador para esto?**
	oon adapta-d*o*r p*a*ra *e*sto
a bottle of butane gas?	**una botella de gas butano?**
	*oo*na bot*e*l-ya deh g*a*s boot*a*n-o
a bottle of propane gas?	**una botella de gas propano?**
	*oo*na bot*e*l-ya deh g*a*s prop*a*n-o
a fuse?	**un fusible?**
	oon foos*ee*bleh
an insecticide spray?	**un insecticida en spray?**
	oon insecti-th*ee*da en spr*a*-ee
a light bulb?	**una bombilla?**
	*oo*na bomb*ee*-ya
The drain	**El desagüe**
	el des-*a*g-we
The toilet	**El servicio**
	el sairb*i*th-yo
... is blocked	**... está atascado**
	... est*a* at-*a*sc*a*do
The sink is blocked	**La fregadera está atascada**
	la freg-ad*ai*ra est*a* at-*a*sc*a*da

The gas is leaking
Hay un escape de gas
ah-ee oon escap-eh deh gas

Can you mend it
straightaway?
¿Puede arreglarlo ahora mismo?
pwed-eh arreglar-lo ah-ora mismo

When can you mend it?
¿Cuándo puede arreglarlo?
cwando pwed-eh arreglar-lo

How much do I owe you?
¿Cuánto le debo?
cwanto leh deb-o

When is the rubbish
collected?
¿Cuándo recogen la basura?
cwando rec-o-hen la basoo-ra

LIKELY REACTIONS

What's your name?
¿Cómo se llama?
com-o seh yama

What's your address?
¿Cuál es su dirección?
cwal es soo dirrek-thion

There's a shop ...
Hay una tienda ...
ah-ee oona tee-enda ...

in town
en la ciudad
en la thee-oodad

in the village
en el pueblo
en el pweb-lo

I can't come ...
No puedo ir ...
no pwed-o eer ...

today
hoy
oy

this week
esta semana
esta sem-anna

until Monday
hasta el lunes
asta el loon-es

I can come ...
Puedo ir ...
pwed-o eer ...

on Tuesday
el martes
el mart-es

when you want
cuando usted quiera
cwando oosted kee-aira

Every day
Cada día
cad-ah deea

Every other day
Un día sin otro
oon deea sin ot-ro

On Wednesdays
Los miércoles
[*For days of the week, p. 135*] los mee-aircol-es

General shopping

The drug store/The chemist's

ESSENTIAL INFORMATION

- Look for the word
  FARMACIA (drug store);
  or these signs.
- Medicines (drugs) are available
  only at a drug store.

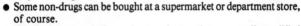

- Some non-drugs can be bought at a supermarket or department store, of course.
- Try the drug store *before* going to a doctor: they are usually qualified to treat minor injuries.
- Normal opening times are 9 a.m. – 1 p.m. and 4 p.m. – 8 p.m.
- If the drug store is shut, a notice on the door headed **FARMACIAS DE GUARDIA** gives the address of the nearest drug store on duty.
- Some toiletries can also be bought at a **PERFUMERIA,** but they will probably be more expensive.
- Finding a drug store, see p. 17.

WHAT TO SAY

I'd like ...	**Quiero ...**
	kee-*airo* ...
some Alka Seltzer	**Alka Seltzer**
	alka selthair
some antiseptic	**antiséptico**
	antiseptico
some aspirin	**aspirinas**
	aspir*in*-as
some bandage	**vendas**
	bend-as
some cotton wool	**algodón**
	algod-*on*
some eye drops	**gotas para los ojos**
	got-as para los *o*-hos

I'd like ...	**Quiero ...**
	kee-*airo* ...
some foot powder	**polvos para los pies**
	pol-bos para los pee-*es*
some gauze dressing	**gasa**
	gas-ah
some inhalant	**inhalante**
	in-a*lan*teh
some insect repellent	**loción contra los insectos**
	loth-*yon* contra los in*sec*tos
some lip salve	**cacao para los labios**
	cac*a*-o para los *lab*-yos
some nose drops	**gotas para la nariz**
	got-as para la nar*eeth*
some sticking plaster	**esparadrapo**
	esparad*rap*po
some throat pastilles	**pastillas para la garganta**
	pas*tee*-yas para la gar*gan*ta
some Vaseline	**Vaselina**
	bas-el-*een*a
I'd like something for ...	**Quiero algo para ...**
	kee-*airo* algo para ...
bites/stings	**las picaduras**
	las pic-ad*oo*ras
burns	**las quemaduras**
	las kem-ad*oo*ras
chilblains	**los sabañones**
	los sab-an-*yon*-es
a cold	**el catarro**
	el cat*a*rro
constipation	**el estreñimiento**
	el estren-yee-mee-*ento*
a cough	**la tos**
	la t*o*s
diarrhoea	**la diarrea**
	la dee-ah-*reh*-ah
ear-ache	**el dolor de oido**
	el dol-*or* deh o-*eedo*
flu	**la gripe**
	la *greep*-eh
scalds	**las escaldaduras**
	las escald-ad*oo*ras

I'd like something for ...	**Quiero algo para ...**
	kee-*air*o *a*lgo p*a*ra ...
sore gums	**el dolor de encías**
	el dol-*o*r deh enth*ee*-as
sprains	**las torceduras**
	las torthed-*oo*ras
sunburn	**las quemaduras de sol**
	las kem-ad*oo*ras deh sol
travel sickness	**el mareo**
	el ma-r*e*yo
I need ...	**Necesito ...**
	neth-es*ee*to ...
some baby food	**comida para niños**
	com-*ee*da p*a*ra n*ee*n-yos
some contraceptives	**anticonceptivos**
	anti-conthept-*ee*bos
some deodorant	**desodorante**
	desodor*a*nteh
some disposable nappies	**pañales de papel**
	pan-y*a*l-es deh pap-*e*l
some handcream	**crema para las manos**
	crem-ah p*a*ra las m*a*n-os
some lipstick	**lápiz de labios**
	l*a*p-ith deh l*a*b-yos
some make-up remover	**crema limpiadora**
	crem-ah limp-yad*o*ra
some paper tissues	**tisús**
	tis*oo*s
some razor blades	**cuchillas**
	cooch*ee*-yas
some safety pins	**imperdibles**
	impaird*ee*-bles
some sanitary towels	**compresas**
	compr*e*s-as
some shaving cream	**crema de afeitar**
	crem-ah deh afeyt*a*r
some soap	**jabón**
	hab-*o*n
some suntan lotion/oil	**loción/aceite bronceador**
	loth-y*o*n/ath*a*y-teh bronteh-ad*o*r
some talcum powder	**polvos de talco**
	p*o*l-bos deh t*a*lco

some Tampax	**Tampax**
	tampax
some (soft) toilet paper	**papel higiénico (suave)**
	pap-el eehi-yennico (swa-beh)
some toothpaste	**pasta de dientes**
[*For other essential*	pasta deh dee-ent-es
expressions, see 'Shop talk', p. 54]	

Holiday items

ESSENTIAL INFORMATION

● Places to shop at and signs to look for:
  LIBRERIA-PAPELERIA (stationery)
  FOTOGRAFIA (films)
  MATERIAL FOTOGRAFICO (films)
  and the main department stores:
  GALERIAS PRECIADOS
  SEPU
  EL CORTE INGLES

WHAT TO SAY

Where can I buy ... ?	**¿Dónde puedo comprar ... ?**
	dondeh pwed-o comprar ...
I'd like ...	**Quiero ...**
	kee-airo ...
a bag	**un bolso**
	oon bolso
a beach ball	**una pelota para la playa**
	oona pelota para la pla-ya
a bucket	**un cubo**
	oon coobo
an English newspaper	**un periódico inglés**
	oon peri-od-ico in-gles
some envelopes	**sobres**
	sob-res

I'd like ...	Quiero ...
	kee-*airo* ...
a guide book	una guía
	*oo*na ghee-a
a map (of the area)	un plano (del área)
	oon plan-o (del *a*-reh-a)
some postcards	postales
	post*a*l-es
a spade	una pala
	*oo*na p*a*l-ah
a straw hat	un sombrero de paja
	oon sombr*airo* deh p*a*-ha
a suitcase	una maleta
	*oo*na malet-ah
some sunglasses	unas gafas de sol
	*oo*nas g*a*f-as deh sol
a sunshade	una sombrilla
	*oo*na sombree-ya
an umbrella	un paraguas
	oon pa-r*a*gwas
some writing paper	papel de escribir
	pap-*e*l deh escrib-*eer*
I'd like ... [*show the camera*]	Quiero ...
	kee-*airo* ...
a colour film	un rollo en color
	oon ro-yo en col-or
a black and white film	un rollo en blanco y negro
	oon ro-yo en bl*a*nco ee neg-ro
for prints	para papel
	p*a*ra pap-*e*l
for slides	para diapositivas
	p*a*ra dee-aposit*ee*bas
12 (24/36) exposures	de doce (veinticuatro/treinta y seis) fotos
	deh d*o*theh (beyntee-cw*a*tro/ treynta-ee-seys) fot-os
a standard 8mm film	un rollo standard de ocho milimetros
	oon ro-yo stan-d*e*rd deh *o*ch-o mil*i*met-ros
a super 8 film	un rollo super ocho
	oon ro-yo s*oo*pair *o*ch-o

some flash bulbs	**unas bombillas de flash**
	oonas bombee-yas deh flash
This camera is broken	**Esta cámara esta rota**
	esta camara esta rot-ah
The film is stuck	**El rollo esta atascado**
	el ro-yo esta atascad-o
Please can you ...	**Por favor, ¿puede ...**
	por fab-or pwed-eh ...
develop/print this?	**revelar/imprimir esto?**
	rebel-ar/imprim-eer esto
load the camera for me?	**recargar mi cámara?**
	rek-argar mee camara

[For other essential expressions, see 'Shop talk', p. 54]

The smoke shop

ESSENTIAL INFORMATION

- Tobacco is sold where you
  see this sign which is red and yellow
- A smoke shop is called
  ESTANCO or
  TABACALERA.
- To ask if there is one near by, see p. 17.
- Smoke shops always sell postage stamps, and you can even mail your letters in some of them.
- They also sell lottery tickets and other items that you usually find in a stationery.
- You can buy cigarettes as well in bars, supermarkets, at newsstands and kiosks.

WHAT TO SAY

A packet of cigarettes ...	**Un paquete de cigarrillos ...**
	oon pak*et*-eh deh thiggar*ee*-yos ...
with filters	**con filtro**
	con f*i*ltro
without filters	**sin filtro**
	sin f*i*ltro
king size	**extra largos**
	*e*xtra *l*argos
menthol	**mentolados**
	mentol*a*d-os
Those up there ...	**Esos de allí ...**
	*e*s-os deh a-y*ee* ...
on the right	**a la derecha**
	ah la der*e*ch-ah
on the left	**a la izquierda**
	ah la ithk-y*air*da
These [*point*]	**Estos**
	*e*stos

Cigarettes, please ...	**Cigarillos, por favor ...**
	thiggar*ee*-yos por fab-*or* ...
100, 200, 300	**cien, doscientos, trescientos**
	thee-*en* dos-thee-*en*tos
	tres-thee-*en*tos
two packets	**dos paquetes**
	dos pak*et*-es
Have you got ...	**¿Tiene ...**
	tee-*en*-eh ...
English cigarettes?	**cigarillos ingleses?**
	thiggar*ee*-yos in-gl*es*-es
American cigarettes?	**cigarrillos americanos?**
	thiggar*ee*-yos americ*an*os
English pipe tobacco?	**tabaco de pipa inglés?**
	tab*a*cco deh p*ee*pa in-gl*es*
American pipe tobacco?	**tabaco de pipa americano?**
	tab*a*cco deh p*ee*pa americ*an*o
rolling tobacco?	**picadura de tabaco?**
	picad*oo*-ra deh tab*a*cco
A packet of pipe tobacco	**Un paquete de tabaco de pipa**
	oon pak*et*-eh deh tab*a*cco deh p*ee*pa
That one down there ...	**Ese de allá abajo ...**
	e*s*-eh deh a-y*a* ab*a*-ho ...
on the right	**a la derecha**
	ah la der*ec*h-ah
on the left	**a la izquierda**
	ah la ithk-y*air*da
This one [*point*]	**Este**
	e*s*teh
A cigar, please	**Un puro, por favor**
	oon p*oo*-ro por fab-*or*
That one [*point*]	**Ese**
	e*s*-eh
Some cigars	**Puros**
	p*oo*-ros
Those [*point*]	**Esos**
	e*s*-os
A box of matches	**Una caja de cerillas**
	*oo*na c*a*-ha deh ther*ee*-yas
A packet of pipe-cleaners [*Show lighter*]	**Un paquete de escobillas**
	oon pak*et*-eh deh escob*ee*-yas

A packet of flints	**Un paquete de piedras de encendedor**
	oon paket-eh deh **pee-edras deh enthendedor**
Lighter fuel	**Combustible para el encendedor**
	comboosteebleh para el enthendedor
Lighter gas, please	**Gas para el encendedor, por favor**
	gas para el enthendedor por fab-or

[For other essential expressions, see 'Shop talk', p. 54]

Buying clothes

ESSENTIAL INFORMATION

- Look for:
  CONFECCIONES SEÑORA (women's clothes)
  SEDERIA (lingerie)
  BOUTIQUE
  MODAS (fashions)
  CONFECCIONES CABALLERO (men's clothes)
  SASTRERIA-PAÑERIA (men's clothes)
  ZAPATERIA/CALZADOS (shoe shop)
- If you are interested in leather and fur articles look for a **PELETERIA** or **CURTIDOS** or **ARTICULOS DE PIEL.**
- You can also buy clothes in the big stores: **ALMACENES** or **GALERIAS.**
- Don't buy without being measured first or without trying things on.
- Don't rely on conversion charts of clothing sizes (see. p. 143).
- If you are buying for someone else, take their measurements with you.

WHAT TO SAY

I'd like ...	Quiero ... kee-*airo* ...
an anorak	un anor*ak* oon anor*ak*
a belt	un cintur*ón* oon thintoo-*ron*
a bikini	un bik*ini* oon bik*ini*
a blouse	una blusa *oo*na bl*oo*sa
a bra	un sujetador oon soohet-ad*or*
a cap (swimming/skiing)	un gorro (de baño/de esquí) oon *gorro* (deh ban-yo/deh sk*í*)
a cardigan	una chaqueta de punto *oo*na chaket-ah deh p*oo*nto
a coat	un abrigo oon abr*ee*go
a dress	un vestido oon best*ee*do
a hat	un sombrero oon sombr*airo*
a jacket	una chaqueta *oo*na chaket-ah
a jumper	un jersey oon hair-s*ay*
a nightdress	un camisón oon camis*on*
a pair of pyjamas	un pijama oon peeh*am*-ah
a pullover	un jersey oon hair-s*ay*
a raincoat	un impermeable oon impairmeh-*ab*-leh
a shirt	una camisa *oo*na cam*ee*sa
a skirt	una falda *oo*na f*al*da
a suit	un traje oon tr*a*-heh

I'd like ...	Quiero ...
	kee-*airo* ...
a swimsuit	un traje de baño
	oon tra-heh deh ban-yo
a T-shirt	una camiseta
	*oo*na cami-set-ah
I'd like a pair of ...	Quiero un par de ...
	kee-*airo* oon par deh ...
briefs (women)	bragas
	br*a*gas
gloves	guantes
	gwan-tes
jeans	vaqueros
	bak-*airo*s
shorts	pantalones cortos
	pantal*o*n-es c*o*rtos
socks (short/long)	calcetines (cortos/largos)
	caltheteen-es (cortos/largos)
stockings	medias
	med-yas
tights	leotardos
	leot*a*rdos
trousers	pantalones
	pantal*o*n-es
underpants (men)	calzoncillos
	calthonth*ee*-yos
I'd like a pair of ...	Quiero un par de ...
	kee-*airo* oon par deh ...
shoes	zapatos
	thap*a*t-os
canvas shoes	zapatos de lona
	thap*a*t-os deh l*o*n-ah
sandals	sandalias
	sand*a*l-yas
beach shoes	playeras
	pla-y*airr*as
smart shoes	zapatos de vestir
	thap*a*t-os deh best*ee*r
boots	botas
	b*o*t-as
moccasins	mocasines
	moccas*i*n-es

My size is ... (clothes)	**Mi talla es ...**
	mee ta-ya es
My size is ... (shoes)	**Mi número es ...**
	mee noomairo es ...
Can you measure me, please?	**¿Puede medirme, por favor?**
	pwed-eh medeermeh por fab-or
Can I try it on?	**¿Puedo probarmelo?**
	pwed-o probarmeh-lo
It's for a present	**Es para un regalo**
	es para oon reg-al-o
These are the measurements ...	**Estas son las medidas ...**
[*Show written*]	estas son las medeedas ...
bust	**busto**
	boosto
chest	**pecho**
	pech-o
collar	**cuello**
	cwel-yo
hip	**cadera**
	cadaira
leg	**pierna**
	pee-airna
waist	**cintura**
	thin-toora
Have you got something ...	**¿Tiene algo ...**
	tee-en-eh algo ...
in black ?	**en negro?**
	en neg-ro
in white?	**en blanco?**
	en blanco
in grey?	**en gris?**
	en grees
in blue?	**en azul?**
	en athool
in brown?	**en marrón?**
	en marron
in pink?	**en rosa?**
	en ros-ah
in green?	**en verde?**
	en bair-deh
in red?	**en rojo?**
	en ro-ho

Have you got something ...	¿Tiene algo ...
	tee-*en*-eh *a*lgo ...
in yellow?	en amarillo?
	en amar*ee*-yo
in this colour? [*point*]	en este color?
	en *e*steh co*l*or
in cotton?	en algodón?
	en algod*o*n
in denim?	en dril?
	en dr*i*l
in leather?	en cuero?
	en cw*ai*ro
in nylon?	en nylon?
	en *n*ylon
in suede?	en ante?
	en *a*nteh
in wool?	en lana?
	en l*a*n-ah
in this material? [*point*]	en este material?
	en *e*steh ma-teri-*a*l

[*For other essential expressions, see 'Shop talk', p. 54*]

Replacing equipment

ESSENTIAL INFORMATION

- Look for these shops and signs:
  FERRETERIA (hardware)
  ELECTRODOMESTICOS (electrical goods)
  DROGUERIA (household cleaning materials)
- In a supermarket or department store look for these signs:
  HOGAR, or ARTICULOS PARA EL HOGAR and
  ARTICULOS DE LIMPIEZA.
- To ask the way to the shop, see p. 17.
- At a campsite try their shop first.

WHAT TO SAY

Have you got ...   ¿Tiene ...
                       tee-*en*-eh ...

an adaptor   **un adaptador?**
[*show appliance*]   oon adapta-dor

a bottle of butane gas?   **una botella de gas butano?**
                          *oo*na botel-ya deh gas bootan-o

a bottle of propane gas?   **una botella de gas propano?**
                           *oo*na botel-ya deh gas propan-o

a bottle opener?   **un abrebotellas?**
                      oon abreh-botel-yas

a corkscrew?   **un sacacorchos?**
                      oon sac-acorchos

any disinfectant?   **desinfectante?**
                      des-infectanteh

any disposable cups? **vasos de papel?**
                      bas-os deh pap-el

any disposable plates?   **platos de papel?**
                         plat-os deh pap-el

a drying up cloth?   **un paño de cocina?**
                      oon pan-yo deh cotheena

any forks?   **tenedores?**
                      ten-ed-or-es

a fuse? [*show old one*]   **un fusible?**
                           oon fooseebleh

an insecticide spray?   **un insecticida en spray?**
                        oon insecti-theeda en spra-ee

a paper kitchen roll?   **un rollo de papel de cocina?**
                        oon ro-yo deh pap-el deh cotheena

any knives?   **cuchillos?**
                      coochee-yos

a light bulb? [*show old   **una bombilla?**
one*]   *oo*na bombee-ya

a plastic bucket?   **un cubo de plástico?**
                      oon coobo deh plastico

a plastic can?   **una lata de plástico?**
                      *oo*na lat-ah deh plastico

a scouring pad?   **un estropajo?**
                      oon estropa-ho

a spanner?   **una llave inglesa?**
                      *oo*na yab-eh in-gles-ah

Have you got . . .	**¿Tiene . . .**
	tee-*en*-eh . . .
a sponge?	**una esponja?**
	*oo*na espong-ha
any string?	**cuerda?**
	cw*air*da
any tent pegs?	**estacas de camping?**
	est*ac*as deh camping
a tin opener?	**un abrelatas?**
	oon abrel-*at*-as
a torch?	**una linterna?**
	*oo*na lint*air*na
any torch batteries?	**pilas de linterna?**
[*show old ones*]	p*ee*las deh lint*air*na
a universal plug (for the sink)?	**un tapón universal (para la fregadera)?**
	oon tap-*on* oonibair-*sal* p*a*ra la freg-ad*air*a
a washing line?	**un tendedero?**
	oon tended-*air*o
any washing powder?	**detergente?**
	det-air-*hen*teh
any washing-up liquid?	**lavavajillas?**
	lababa-*hee*-yas
a washing-up brush?	**un cepillo para fregar los platos?**
[*For other essential expressions, see 'Shop talk', p. 54*]	oon the*pee*-yo p*a*ra freg*a*r los plat-os

Shop talk

ESSENTIAL INFORMATION

● Know your coins and bills
coins: see illustration
bills: 100 pesetas, 500, 1000 and 5000 pesetas

● Know how to say the important weights and measures

50 grams	**cincuenta gramos**
	thin-cwenta gram-os
100 grams	**cien gramos**
	thee-en gram-os
200 grams	**doscientos gramos**
	dos-thee-entos gram-os
½ kilo	**medio kilo**
	med-yo kílo
1 kilo	**un kilo**
	oon kílo
2 kilos	**dos kilos**
	dos kílos
½ litre	**medio litro**
	med-yo litro
1 litre	**un litro**
	oon litro
2 litres	**dos litros**
[For numbers, see p. 131]	dos litros

● In small shops don't be surprised if the customers, as well as the shop assistant, say 'hello' and 'good-bye' to you.

Customer

Hello	**Hola**
	o-la
Good morning	**Buenos días**
	bwen-os deeas
Good afternoon	**Buenas tardes**
	bwen-as tard-es
Good-bye	**Adiós**
	ad-yos
I'm just looking	**Sólo estoy mirando**
	sol-o estoy mirrando
Excuse me	**Perdone**
	pairdon-eh
How much is this/that?	**¿Cuánto es esto/eso?**
	cwanto es esto/es-o
What is that?	**¿Qué es eso?**
	keh es es-o
What are those?	**¿Qué son esos?**
	keh son es-os
Is there a discount?	**¿Hay descuento?**
	ah-ee des-cwento

I'd like that, please	**Quiero eso, por favor** kee-*airo* es-o por fab-*or*
Not that	**Eso no** es-o no
Like that	**Así** a*see*
That's enough, thank you	**Basta, gracias** b*asta* gr*ath*-yas
More, please	**Mas, por favor** m*as* por fab-*or*
Less, please	**Menos, por favor** men-os por fab-*or*
That's fine	**Eso está bien** es-o est*a* bee-en
OK	**Está bien** est*a* bee-en
I won't take it, thank you	**No lo tomo, gracias** no lo tom-o gr*ath*-yas
It's not right	**No está bien** no est*a* bee-en
Thank you very much	**Muchas gracias** m*oo*chas gr*ath*-yas
Have you got something ...	**¿Tiene algo ...** tee-en-eh *algo* ...
better?	**mejor?** m*eh*-hor
cheaper?	**mas barato?** m*as* ba-r*at*-o
different?	**diferente?** diffair-enteh
larger?	**mas grande?** m*as* grandeh
smaller?	**mas pequeño?** m*as* peken-yo
At what time do you ...	**¿A qué hora ...** ah keh *ora* ...
open?	**abren?** *ab*-ren
close?	**cierran?** thee-erran
Can I have a bag, please?	**¿Puedo tener una bolsa, por favor?** pwed-o ten-*air* *oo*na bolsa por fab-*or*

Can you give me a receipt?	**¿Puede darme un recibo?** pwed-eh darmeh oon retheebo
Do you take ...	**¿Toman ustedes ...** tom-an oosted-es ...
English/American money?	**dinero inglés/americano?** din-airo in-gles/american**o**
travellers' cheques?	**cheques de viaje?** ch**e**k-es deh bee-ah-heh
credit cards?	**tarjetas de crédito?** tarhet-as deh credit-**o**
I'd like ...	**Quiero ...** kee-airo ...
one like that	**uno así** **oo**no asee
two like that	**dos así** dos asee

Shop assistant

Can I help you?	**¿En qué puedo servirle?** en keh pwed-o sairbeer-leh
What would you like?	**¿Qué desea/quiere?** keh des-eh-ah/kee-aireh
Will that be all?	**¿Será eso todo?** serra es-o tod-o
Is that all?	**¿Eso es todo?** es-o es tod-o
Anything else?	**¿Algo mas?** algo mas
Would you like it wrapped?	**¿Quiere que se lo envuelva?** kee-aireh keh seh lo enbwelba
Sorry, none left	**Lo siento, no queda ninguno** lo see-ento no ked-ah nin-g**oo**no
I haven't got any	**No tengo** no tengo
I haven't got any more	**No tengo mas** no tengo mas
How many do you want?	**¿Cuántos quiere?** cwantos kee-aireh
How much do you want?	**¿Cuánto quiere?** cwanto kee-aireh
Is that enough?	**¿Basta?** basta

Shopping for food

Bread

ESSENTIAL INFORMATION

- Finding a baker's, see p. 17.
- Key words to look for:
  HORNO (baker's)
  PANADERIA (baker's)
  PANADERO (baker)
  PAN (bread)
- Supermarkets of any size and general stores nearly always sell bread.
- **Panaderías**, as well as other shops, are open from 9 a.m. – 1 p.m. and from 4 p.m. – 8 p.m. closing at lunchtime. In popular resorts, the shops often remain open all day.
- The most characteristic type of loaf is the **barra** which is a wider version of the 'french stick', and comes in different sizes according to the weight.
- For any other type of loaf, say **un pan** (oon p*a*n), and point.
- In some bakers' you can buy milk; look for this sign: **LECHERIA-PANADERIA**. Soft drinks, sweets and ice-creams can also be bought here.
- It's quite usual in Spain to have your bread delivered; if you wish to take advantage of this service, simply have a word with your local baker. You only have to say: **¿Puede traer el pan a casa?** (pwed-eh tra-*air* el p*a*na c*a*s-a).

WHAT TO SAY

Some bread, please	**Pan, por favor** p*a*n for fab-*or*
A loaf (like that)	**Un pan (así)** oon p*a*n (as*ee*)
One long loaf	**Una barra** *oo*na b*a*rra
Three loaves	**Tres panes** tres p*a*n-es

Four long loaves	**Cuatro barras**
	cwatro barras
250 grams of ...	**Doscientos cincuenta gramos de ...**
	dos-thee-entos thin-cwenta ...
	gram-os deh ...
½ kilo of ...	**Medio kilo de ...**
	med-yo kilo deh ...
1 kilo of ...	**Un kilo de ...**
	oon kilo deh ...
A bread roll	**Un panecillo**
	oon pannethee-yo
Four bread rolls	**Cuatro panecillos**
	cwatro pannethee-yos
Four crescent rolls	**Cuatro croissants**
	cwatro crwassans
A packet of ...	**Un paquete de ...**
	oon paket-eh deh ...
English bread	**pan de molde**
	pan deh moldeh
toasted bread	**pan tostado**
	pan tostad-o
brown bread	**pan integral**
	pan inteh-gral

[For other essential expressions, see 'Shop talk', p. 54]

Cakes

ESSENTIAL INFORMATION

- Key words to look for:
  PASTELERÍA (cake shop)
  CONFITERÍA (confectionery, they also sell cakes)
  PASTELERO (cake/pastry maker)
  PASTELES (cakes)
  PASTAS (pastries)
- **CHURRERÍA**: a place to buy churros, a kind of fritter that can be eaten on its own (takeaway) or dipped in hot thick chocolate. You have to ask for: chocolate con churros.
- **CAFETERÍA**: a place where you can buy cakes, as well as drinks. You can also have chocolate and churros. See p. 80 'Ordering a drink'.
- To find a cake shop, see p. 17

WHAT TO SAY

The type of cakes you find in the shops varies from region to region but the following are some of the most common.

un churro	a finger-size fritter
oon cho*oro*	
un buñuelo	a round fritter
oon boon-yoo-*el*-o	
magdalenas	madeleines (small sponge
magda-*len*-as	teacakes)
una ensaimada	a bun made of puff pastry covered
oona en-sa-ee-m*ad*-ah	with sugar icing and filled with
	cream
mantecado	shortbread
el manteh-c*ad*-o	
turrón	nougat (can be hard or soft)
too-*ron*	
el mazapán	marzipan
el matha-p*an*	
una yema	a candied egg yolk
oona *yem*-ah	

una rosquilla a ring-shaped roll (like a
oona ros-*kee*-ya doughnut)
un merengue a meringue
oon meh-*ren*-geh

You usually buy medium-size cakes by number:

one doughnut **un donut**
oon don-*oot*
two doughnuts, please **dos donuts, por favor**
dos don-*oots* por fab-*or*

You buy small cakes by weight:

200 grams of cream puffs **doscientos gramos de pastelitos
de crema**
dos-thee-*en*tos *gram*-os deh
pastel-*eet*os deh crem-*ah*
400 grams of biscuits **cuatrocientos gramos de galletas**
cwatro-thee-*en*tos *gram*-os deh
ga-yet-as

You may want to buy a larger cake by the slice:

one slice of apple cake **un trozo de pastel de manzana**
oon *troth*-o deh *pastel* deh
manth*ana*
two slices of almond cake **dos trozos de pastel de almendra**
dos *troth*-os deh *pastel* deh
almendra

You buy **churros** by pesetas:

20 pesetas of churros, please **veinte pesetas de churros, por
favor**
b*eyn*-teh pes-*et*-as deh ch*oo*-ros
por fab-*or*

You may also want to say:

a selection, please **pasteles variados, por favor**
pastel-es baree-*ad*-os por fab-*or*

[*For other essential expressions, see 'Shop talk', p. 54*]

Ice-cream and sweets

ESSENTIAL INFORMATION

- Key words to look for:
  HELADOS (ice-creams)
  HELADERO (ice-cream maker/seller)
  HELADERIA (ice-cream shop/parlour)
  HORCHATERIA (ice-cream shop which also sells soft ice drinks)
  CONFITERIA (sweet and cake shop)
  BOMBONERIA (sweet shop)
  CONFITERO (sweet maker/seller)
  PASTELERIA (cake shop)
  PASTELERO (cake/pastry maker)
- Best known ice-cream brand names:

FRIGO	**LAR**
CAMI	**LIC**
LIDO	**ITALIANOS**

- Prepacked sweets are available in general stores and supermarkets and usually in **PANADERIAS** (bakers'), where you can also buy ice-creams.
- You can also buy sweets in kiosks and in the tobacconist's.

WHAT TO SAY

A ... ice, please	**Un helado de ... , por favor**
	oon el*a*d-o d*ə*h ... por fab-*or*
chocolate	**chocolate**
	chocol*a*t-eh
pistachio	**mantecado**
	manteh-c*a*d-o
raspberry	**frambuesa**
	frambw*e*ssa
strawberry	**fresa**
	fr*e*ssa
vanilla	**vainilla**
	ban*ee*-ya
coffee	**café**
	caf*e*h

A ... ice, please	**Un helado de ... , por favor**
	oon elad-o deh ... por fab-or
nougat flavour	**turrón**
	too-ron
lemon	**limón**
	lim-on
orange	**naranja**
	na-rang-ha
tuttifrutti	**tuttifrutti**
	toottifrootti
creamy	**nata**
	na-ta
hazelnut	**avellana**
	ab-el-yanna
mint	**menta**
	menta
croccanti	**croccanti**
	croccanti
A single	**Uno sencillo**
[specify flavour as above]	oono senthee-yo
Two singles	**Dos sencillos**
	dos senthee-yos
A double	**Uno doble**
	oono dobleh
Two doubles	**Dos dobles**
	dos dobles
A cone	**Un barquillo**
	oon barkee-yo
An iced lolly	**Un polo**
	oon pol-o
A chocolate iced lolly	**Un polo de bombón**
	oon pol-o de bombon
A wafer	**Un corte**
	oon corteh
A lollipop	**Un pirulí**
	oon piroolee
A tub	**Un Cami**
	oon ca-mee
A cake with ice-cream	**Una tarta helada**
	oona tarta eladda
A packet of ...	**Un paquete de ... .**
	oon paket-eh deh ...
chewing gum	**chicle**
	chee-cleh

100 grams of ...	**Cien gramos de ...**
	thee-*en* gram-os deh ...
200 grams of ...	**Doscientos gramos de ...**
	dos-thee-*entos* gram-os deh ...
sweets	**caramelos**
	caramel-os
toffees	**pastillas de café con leche**
	pas*tee*-yas deh cafeh con lech-eh
chocolates	**bombones**
	bombon-es
mints	**caramelos de menta**
[*For other essential*	caramel-os deh menta
expressions, see 'Shop talk', p. 54]	

In the supermarket

ESSENTIAL INFORMATION

● The place to ask for: [*see p. 17*]

UN SUPERMERCADO (supermarket)
UN AUTOSERVICIO (corner self-service)
ALIMENTACION GENERAL (general food store)
● You may see outside the shop the words: **SPAR** or **VEGE.**
● Key instructions on signs in the shop:
ENTRADA (entrance)
PROHIBIDA LA ENTRADA (no entry)
SALIDA (exit)
PROHIBIDA LA SALIDA (no exit)
SIN SALIDA (no way out)
SALIDA SIN COMPRAS (exit for non-buyers)
CAJA (check-out, cash desk)
EN OFERTA (on offer)
AUTOSERVICIO (self-service)
● Supermarkets are open from 9 a.m. – 1 p.m. and from 4 p.m. – 8 p.m., but in some places, especially in holiday resorts and in the summer, supermarkets, as well as other shops, stay open at lunchtime.
● No need to say anything in a supermarket, but ask if you can't see what you want.

WHAT TO SAY

Excuse me, please	**Perdone, por favor**
	pairdon-eh por fab-or
Where is ...	**¿Dónde está ...**
	dondeh esta ...
the bread?	**el pan?**
	el pan
the butter?	**la mantequilla?**
	la manteh-kee-ya
the cheese?	**el queso?**
	el kes-o
the chocolate?	**el chocolate?**
	el chocolat-eh
the coffee?	**el café?**
	el cafeh
the cooking oil?	**el aceite?**
	el athay-teh
the fish (fresh)?	**el pescado?**
	el pescad-o
the fruit?	**la fruta?**
	la froota
the jam?	**la mermelada?**
	la mairmel-ad-ah
the meat?	**la carne?**
	la carneh
the milk?	**la leche?**
	la lech-eh
the mineral water?	**el agua mineral?**
	el agwa mineral
the salt?	**la sal?**
	la sal
the sugar?	**el azúcar?**
	el athoocar
the tea?	**el té?**
	el teh
the tinned fish?	**el pescado en lata?**
	el pescad-o en lat-ah
the tinned fruit?	**la fruta en lata?**
	la froota en lat-ah
the vinegar?	**el vinagre?**
	el beenag-reh

the wine?	**el vino?**
	el b*ee*no
the yogurt?	**el yogurt?**
	el yog*oo*rt
Where are ...	**¿Dónde están ...**
	d*o*ndeh est*a*n ...
the biscuits?	**las galletas?**
	las ga-y*e*ttas
the crisps?	**las patatas fritas?**
	las pat*a*t-as fr*ee*tas
the eggs?	**los huevos?**
	los w*e*b-os
the frozen foods?	**los congelados?**
	los conhell*a*d-os
the fruit juices?	**los zumos de fruta?**
	los th*oo*m-os deh fr*oo*ta
the pastas?	**las pastas?**
	las p*a*stas
the seafoods?	**los mariscos?**
	los ma-r*i*skos
the snails?	**los caracoles?**
	los caracol-es
the soft drinks?	**las bebidas sin alcohol?**
	las beb*ee*das sin alco-*o*l
the sweets?	**los caramelos?**
	los caramel-os
the tinned vegetables?	**las verduras en lata?**
	las bairdoo-ras en lat-ah
the vegetables?	**las verduras?**
	las bairdoo-ras

[For other essential expressions, see 'Shop talk', p. 54]

Picnic food

ESSENTIAL INFORMATION

- Key words to look for:
  CHARCUTERIA (pork butcher's delicatessen)
  EMBUTIDOS (cold meat sausages)
  FIAMBRES (cold meat, cold cuts)
  TIENDA DE ULTRAMARINOS (grocer's)
  MANTEQUERIA (delicatessen)
  CARNECERIA (butcher's)
- In these shops you can buy a wide variety of food such as ham, salami, cheese, olives, appetizers, sausages and freshly made takeaway dishes. Specialities differ from region to region.
- Weight guide:
  4–6oz/150g of prepared salad per two people, if eaten as a starter to a substantial meal.
  3–4oz/100g of prepared salad per person, if eaten as the main part of a picnic-type meal.

WHAT TO SAY

A slice of ...	Una rodaja de ... *oo*na rod-*a*ha deh ...
Two slices of ...	Dos rodajas de ... dos rod-*a*has deh ...
salami	salchichón salcheech*o*n
spicy hard sausage	chorizo chor-*ee*tho
pâté	paté pat*e*h
ham	jamón de york ham-*o*n deh y*o*rk
cured ham, thinly sliced	jamón serrano ham-*o*n serr*a*nnɔ
pork and beef cold meat	mortadela morta-d*e*lla

stuffed turkey	**pavo trufado**
	pab-o troofad-o
100 grams of ...	**Cien gramos de ...**
	thee-en gram-os deh ...
150 grams of ...	**Ciento cincuenta gramos de ...**
	thee-ento thin-cwenta gram-os deh ...
200 grams of ...	**Doscientos gramos de ...**
	dos-thee-entos gram-os deh ...
300 grams of ...	**Trescientos gramos de ...**
	tres-thee-entos gram-os deh ...
Russian salad	**ensalada rusa**
	ensalad-ah roosa
tomato salad	**ensalada de tomate**
	ensalad-ah deh tomat-eh
olives	**olivas**
	oleebas
anchovies	**anchoas**
	ancho-as
cheese	**queso**
	kes-o

You may also like to try some of these:

pizza	pizza
pizza	
salchicha de frankfurt	frankfurter
salcheecha deh frankfort	
pollo asado	roast chicken
pol-yo asad-o	
morcilla	black pudding
morthee-ya	
palitos de queso	cheese sticks
paleetos deh kes-o	
cortezas	pork crackling/scratchings
corteth-as	
puntas de espárragos	asparagus tips
poontas deh esparagos	
salmón ahumado	smoked salmon
sal-mon ah-oomad-o	
butifarra	spiced sausage
booti-farra	
longaniza	highly-seasoned sausage made
longa-neetha	with pork and herbs

olivas rellenas	stuffed olives
ol*ee*bas reh-*yen*-as	
olivas negras	black olives
ol*ee*bas neg-ras	
patatas fritas	crisps
pat*a*t-as fr*ee*tas	
pepinillos	gherkins
peppin*ee*-yos	
galletas saladas	crackers
ga-*yet*-as sal*a*d-as	
sardinas en aceite	sardines in oil
sard*ee*nas en ath*a*y-teh	
sardinas rancias	dry salty sardines
sard*ee*nas *ra*nth-yas	
atún	tuna
at*oo*n	
queso de Burgos	soft, creamy cheese
kes-o deh b*oo*rgos	
queso manchego	hard cheese from ewe's milk
kes-o manch*e*g-o	
queso de roncal	salted, smoked cheese made from
kes-o deh ronc*a*l	ewe's milk
queso de bola	a round-shaped, mild cheese
kes-o deh b*o*l-ah	
queso de cabra	goat cheese
kes-o deh c*a*bra	
queso de teta	a firm, bland cheese made from
kes-o deh teta	cow's milk

[*For other essential expressions, see 'Shop talk', p. 54*]

Fruit and vegetables

ESSENTIAL INFORMATION

- Key words to look for: **VERDURA** (vegetables)
  FRUTA (fruit)   **LEGUMBRES** (vegetables)
  FRUTERO (fruit seller) **VERDULERIA** (vegetable shop)
  FRUTERIA (fruit shop) **FRESCO** (an indication of freshness)
- If possible, buy fruit and vegetables in the market where they are cheaper and fresher than in the shops. Open-air markets are held once or twice a week in most areas (or daily in large towns), usually in the mornings.
- It is customary for you to choose your own fruit and vegetables in the market (and in some shops) and for the stallholder to weigh and price them. You must take your own shopping bag: paper and plastic bags are not normally provided.
- Weight guide: 1 kilo of potatoes is sufficient for six people for one meal.

WHAT TO SAY

½ kilo (1lb) of ...	**Medio kilo de ...**
	med-yo *ki*lo deh ...
1 kilo of ...	**Un kilo de ...**
	oon *ki*lo deh ...
2 kilos of ...	**Dos kilos de ...**
	dos *ki*los deh ...
apples	**manzanas**
	man*tha*nas
bananas	**plátanos**
	p*lat*tan-os
cherries	**cerezas**
	the*reth*-as
figs	**higos**
	ee-gos
grapes (black/white)	**uvas (blancas/negras)**
	*oo*bas (blancas/neg-ras)
oranges	**naranjas**
	na-*rang*-has
pears	**peras**
	*per*ras

2 kilos of ...	**D**os kilos de ...
	dos kilos deh ...
peaches	melocotones
	mellocoton-es
plums	ciruelas
	theer-rwellas
strawberries	fresas
	fressas
A pineapple, please	**U**na piña, por favor
	oona peen-ya por fab-or
A grapefruit	**U**n pomelo
	oon pomello
A melon	**U**n melón
	oon melon
A water-melon	**U**na sandía
	oona sandeea
250 grams of ...	**D**oscientos cincuenta gramos de ...
	dos-thee-entos thin-cwenta gram-os deh ...
½ kilo of ...	**M**edio kilo de ...
	med-yo kilo deh ...
1 kilo of ...	**U**n kilo de ...
	oon kilo deh ...
1½ kilos of ...	**U**n kilo y medio de ...
	oon kilo ee med-yo deh ...
2 kilos of ...	**D**os kilos de ...
	dos kilos deh ...
artichokes	alcachofas
	alkachoffas
asparagus	esparrago
	esparrago
broad beans	habas
	abbas
carrots	zanahorias
	thanna-oree-as
green beans	judías verdes
	hoodee-as bair-des
leeks	puerros
	pwerros
mushrooms	champiñones
	champin-yon-es

onions	**cebollas**
	theb*o*l-yas
peas	**guisantes**
	ghiss*a*nt-es
potatoes	**patatas**
	pat*a*t-as
shallots	**chalotes**
	chall*o*t-es
spinach	**espinacas**
	espin*a*c-as
tomatoes	**tomates**
	tom*a*t-es
A bunch of ...	**Un puñado de ...**
	oon poon-y*a*d-o deh ...
parsley	**perejil**
	perreh*i*l
radishes	**rábanos**
	r*a*b-annos
A head of garlic	**Una cabeza de ajo**
	*o*ona cabeth-ah deh *a*h-ho
A lettuce	**Una lechuga**
	oona lech*oo*ga
A cauliflower	**Una coliflor**
	*o*ona collifl*o*r
A cabbage	**Un repollo**
	oon rep*o*l-yo
A cucumber	**Un pepino**
	oon pep*ee*no
Like that, please	**Así, por favor**
	as*ee* por fab-*o*r

Some fruit and vegetables with which you may not be familiar:

acelgas	chard, a kind of beet with edible
ath*e*lgas	stalks and leaves
calabaza	pumpkin, orange coloured fruit
calab*a*tha	with edible layer next to rind
caqui	date plum: soft sweet winter
c*a*-kee	fruit like a large tomato
escarola	endive, a salad plant, also called
escarol-ah	'chicory'
granada	pomegranate, a fruit, orange in
gran*a*d-ah	colour, with lots of seeds

higo chumbo	prickly pear, as its name suggests,
ee-go ch*oo*mbo	the fruit of a cactus
membrillo	quince, a pear shaped fruit used as
membr*ee*-yo	a preserve
níspero	medlar/loquat, small, slightly
n*ee*spero	sour fruit, orange in colour and
	juicy

[*For other essential expressions, see 'Shop talk', p. 54*]

Meat

ESSENTIAL INFORMATION

- Key words to look for:
  CARNECERIA (butcher's)
  CARNICERO (butcher)
- Weight guide: 4–6oz/125–200g of meat per person for one meal.
- The diagrams opposite are to help you make sense of labels on counters and supermarket displays, and decide which cut or joint to have. Translations do not help, and you don't need to say the Spanish word involved.

WHAT TO SAY

For a joint, choose the type of meat and then say how many people it is for:

Some beef, please	**Buey, por favor**
	b*way* por fab*o*r
Some lamb/young lamb	**Cordero/ternasco**
	cord*ai*ro/tairn*a*sco
Some mutton	**Carnero/oveja**
	carn*ai*ro/ob*e*h-ha

Beef Buey

1 Cuello
2 Espaldilla
3 Pecho
4 Morcillo
5 Lomo alto
6 Solomillo
7 Lomo bajo
8 Tapa
9 Cadera
10 Redondo
11 Contra
12 Babilla
13 Falda con costillar
14 Culeta

Veal Ternera

1 Lomo
2 Cuello
3 Espaldilla
4 Aleta o pecho
5 Falda
6 Riñonada
7 Cadera
8 Babilla
9 Contra
10 Morcillo (osso bucco)

Pork Cerdo

1 Aguja
2 Paletilla
3 Tocino
4 Chuletas o cinta
5 Magro para salchichas
6 Panceta
7 Jamón
8 Manos

Mutton Carnero/Oveja

1 Lomo
2 Costillar
3 Falda
4 Pecina
5 Paletilla
6 Cuello
7 Manos

Some pork	**Cerdo** t*hair*do
Some veal	**Ternera** tairn*aira*
A joint ...	**Un asado ...** oon as*a*do ...
for two people	**para dos personas** p*a*ra dos pairs*o*n-as
for four people	**para cuatro personas** p*a*ra cw*a*tro pairs*o*n-as
for six people	**para seis personas** p*a*ra s*e*ys pairs*o*n-as

For steak, liver or kidneys, do as above:

Some steak, please	**Bistec, por favor** bistec por fab-*o*r
Some liver	**Hígado** *ee*ga-do
Some kidneys	**Riñones** rin-yon-es
Some sausages	**Salchichas** salch*ee*chas
Some mince ...	**Carne picada ...** c*a*rneh peec*a*da ...
for three people	**para tres personas** p*a*ra tres pairs*o*n-as
for five people	**para cinco personas** p*a*ra th*i*nko pairs*o*n-as

For chops do it this way:

Two veal escalopes	**Dos escalopes de ternera** dos escalop-es deh tairn*aira*
Three pork chops	**Tres chuletas de cerdo** tres chool*e*ttas deh t*hair*do
Four mutton chops	**Cuatro chuletas de oveja** cw*a*tro chool*e*ttas deh ob*e*h-ha
Five lamb chops	**Cinco chuletas de cordero** th*i*nko chool*e*ttas deh cord*air*o

You may also want:

A chicken	**Un pollo** oon p*o*l-yo

A rabbit	**Un conejo** oon conneh-ho
A tongue	**Una lengua** oona len-gwa

Other essential expressions [*see also p. 54*]

Please can you ...	**Por favor, ¿puede usted ...** por fab-or pwed-eh oosted ...
mince it?	**picarlo?** peecarlo
dice it?	**cortarlo en trozos?** cortarlo en troth-os
trim the fat?	**quitar la grasa?** keetar la grassa

Fish

ESSENTIAL INFORMATION

- The place to ask for:
  UNA PESCADERIA (fish shop)
- Markets and large supermarkets usually have a fresh fish stall.
- Another key word to look for is MARISCOS (seafood)
- Weight guide: 8oz/250g minimum per person, for one meal,
  of fish bought on the bone.
  i.e. ½ kilo/500g   for 2 people
  1 kilo   for 4 people
  1½ kilos   for 6 people

WHAT TO SAY

Purchase large fish and small shellfish by weight:

½ kilo of ...	**Medio kilo de ...** med-yo kilo deh ...
1 kilo of ...	**Un kilo de ...** oon kilo deh ...

1½ kilos of ...	**Un kilo y medio de ...**
	oon *kílo* ee m*ed*-yo deh ...
clams	**almejas**
	alm*eh*-has
cod	**bacalao**
	bakkal*a*-o
hake	**merluza**
	mairl*oo*tha
mussels	**mejillones**
	mehee-y*on*-es
prawns	**gambas**
	g*a*mbas
sardines	**sardinas**
	sard*ee*nas
shrimps (two names)	**camarones/quisquillas**
	cammar*on*-es/kisk*ee*-yas
sprats	**sardinetas**
	sardin*e*ttas
turbot	**rodaballo**
	roddab*a*-yo
whitebait	**boquerones**
	bokeh-r*on*-es

Some large fish can be purchased by the slice:

One slice of ...	**Una rodaja de ...**
	*oo*na rodd*a*-ha deh ...
Two slices of ...	**Dos rodajas de ...**
	dos rodd*a*-has deh ...
Six slices of ...	**Seis rodajas de ...**
	s*ey*s rodd*a*-has deh ...
salmon	**salmón**
	sal-m*on*
cod	**bacalao**
	bakkal*a*-o
fresh tuna	**bonito**
	bon*ee*to
sea bream	**besugo**
	bes*oo*go

For some shellfish and 'frying pan' fish, specify the number:

A crab, please	**Un cangrejo, por favor** *oo*n cangreh-ho por fab-*or*
A lobster	**Una langosta** *oo*na lan-gosta
A plaice	**Un gallo** oon g*a*l-yo
A whiting	**Una pescadilla** *oo*na pescad*ee*-ya
A trout	**Una trucha** *oo*na tr*oo*cha
A sole	**Un lenguado** oon len-gw*a*ddo
A mackerel	**Una caballa** *oo*na cab*a*l-ya
A herring	**Un arenque** oon arrenkeh
An octopus	**Un pulpo** oon *poo*lpo
A carp	**Una carpa** *oo*na c*a*rpa

Other essential expressions [*see also p. 54*]

Please can you ...	**Por favor, ¿puede ...** por fab-*or* pwed-eh ...
take the heads off?	quitar las cabezas? keet*a*r las cab-*eth*-as
clean them?	limpiarlos? limp-y*a*r-los
fillet them?	quitar la espina? keet*a*r la esp*ee*na

Eating and drinking out

Ordering a drink

ESSENTIAL INFORMATION

- The places to ask for: [see p. 17]
  UNA CAFETERIA (a more luxurious and modern café)
  UN CAFÉ
  UN BAR
- If you want to try Spanish wine and tapas in a typically Spanish atmosphere the places to go are: UNA TASCA, UNA BODEGA, UN MESON or UNA TABERNA. Usually you'll find all these places in the same area and it is the custom to make a tour of several local bars having one or two drinks in each.
- By law, the price list of drinks (TARIFA or LISTA DE PRECIOS) must be displayed outside or in the window.
- There is waiter service in all cafés, but you can drink at the bar or counter if you wish (cheaper).
- Always leave a tip of 10% to 15% of the bill unless you see SERVICIO INCLUIDO, although it is still common practice to leave a few pesetas for these bills also.
- Cafés serve non-alcoholic drinks and alcoholic drinks, and are normally open all day.
- You will find plates of assorted food, e.g. cheese, fish, olives, salads etc. on the bar, usually before lunchtime or dinner time. These are called tapas, and you can either have a portion (una ración, rath-yon) or food on sticks (banderillas, banderee-yas). You have them as an apéritif or a snack with your drink. As with drinks you pay for tapas on leaving the bar, though some offer small tapas free.

WHAT TO SAY

I'd like ... please	Quiero ... por favor
	kee-airo ... por fab-or
a black coffee	un café solo
	oon cafeh sol-o

a white coffee	**un café con leche**
	oon caf*e*h con lech-**eh**
a black coffee with a dash of milk	**un cortado**
	oon cort*a*d-**o**
a tea	**un té**
	oon teh
with milk	**con leche**
	con lech-**eh**
with lemon	**con limón**
	con lim-*on*
a glass of milk	**un vaso de leche**
	oon b*a*sso deh lech-**eh**
a hot chocolate (thick)	**un chocolate**
	oon chocol*a*t-**eh**
a mineral water	**un agua mineral**
	oon *a*gwa miner*a*l
a lemonade	**una limonada**
	oona lim-onn*a*d-**ah**
a Coca Cola	**una Coca Cola**
	*oo*na coca cola
an orangeade	**una naranjada**
	oona na-rang-h*a*dda
an orange juice	**un zumo de naranja**
	oon th*oo*mo deh na-r*a*ng-ha
a grape juice	**un mosto**
	oon m*o*sto
a pineapple juice	**un zumo de piña**
	oon th*oo*mo deh p*i*n-**ya**
a milkshake	**un batido**
	oon bat*ee*do
a beer	**una cerveza**
	*oo*na thairb*e*th-**ah**
a draught beer	**una caña**
	*oo*na c*a*n-**ya**
a cider	**una sidra**
	*oo*na s*i*dra
A glass of ...	**Un vaso de ...**
	oon b*a*sso deh ...
Two glasses of ...	**Dos vasos de ...**
	dos b*a*ssos deh ...
red wine	**vino tinto**
	b*ee*no t*i*nto

Two glasses of ...	**Dos vasos de ...**
	dos bassos deh ...
white wine	**vino blanco**
	beeno blanco
rosé wine	**vino rosado**
	beeno rosad-o
claret wine	**vino clarete**
	beeno claret-eh
dry	**seco**
	sec-o
sweet	**dulce**
	dool-theh
sparkling wine	**vino espumoso**
	beeno espoomoso
champagne	**champán**
	champan
sherry	**jerez**
	herreth
A whisky	**Un whisky**
	oon whisky
with ice	**con hielo**
	con yello
with water	**con agua**
	con agwa
with soda	**con soda**
	con soda
A gin	**Una ginebra**
	oona hinnebra
and tonic	**con tonica**
	con tonica
with lemon	**con limón**
	con lim-on
A brandy/cognac	**Un coñac**
	oon con-yac
A crème de menthe	**Una crema de menta**
	oona crem-ah deh menta
A coffee liqueur	**Una crema de café**
	oona crem-ah deh cafeh
A rum	**Un ron**
	oon ron
A rum coke	**Un Cuba libre**
	oon cooba leebreh

These are local drinks you may like to try:

un anis	aniseed liqueur, served after
oon anees	meals or with biscuits
un granizado	an iced drink, available in a
oon graneethad-o	variety of flavours
una horchata	drink made of nuts, water and
oona orchat-ah	sugar
una manzanilla	similar to sherry but lighter
oona manthanee-ya	it's an apéritif
un moscatel	a sweet wine, served with
oon mosca-tel	desserts and sweets or biscuits
un ponche	punch, usually served after meals
oon ponch-eh	with the coffee
una sangria	made of red wine, bitter lemon
oona sangreea	brandy and sugar – can be
	drunk at any time, even with
	meals
vino de Malaga	sweet wine, an apéritif
beeno deh malaga	
vino quinado	sweet wine made of quinine –
beeno kinnad-o	it's an appetiser
crema de cacao	spirit made of cocoa, taken after
crem-ah deh caca-o	meals or with the dessert

Other essential expressions:

Miss! [*This does not sound abrupt in Spanish*]	**¡Señorita!**
	sen-yoreeta
Waiter!	**¡Camarero!**
	camma-rairo
The bill, please	**La cuenta, por favor**
	la cwenta por fab-or
How much does that come to?	**¿Cuánto es?**
	cwanto es
Is service included?	**¿Está el servicio incluido?**
	esta el sairbith-yo incloo-eedo
Where is the toilet, please?	**¿Dónde están los servicios, por favor?**
	dondeh estan los sairbith-yos por fab-or

Ordering a snack

ESSENTIAL INFORMATION

- Look for a café or bar with these signs:
  TAPAS (appetisers)
  BOCADILLOS (sandwiches)
  MERIENDAS (snacks and meals in the afternoon)
- Look for the names of snacks (listed below) on signs in the window or on the pavement.
- In some regions mobile vans sell hot snacks.
- For cakes, see p. 61.
- For ice-cream, see p. 63.
- For picnic-type snacks, see p. 68.

WHAT TO SAY

I'd like . . . please	Quiero . . . por favor
	kee-*air*o . . . por fab-*or*
a cheese sandwich	un bocadillo de queso
	oon boccad*ee*-yo deh k*es*-o
a ham sandwich	un bocadillo de jamón de york
	oon boccad*ee*-yo deh ham-*on* deh york
a smoked ham sandwich	un bocadillo de jamón serrano
	oon boccad*ee*-yo deh ham-*on* serr*an*no

These are some other snacks you may like to try:

albondigas con tomate	spiced meatballs in tomato sauce
alb*on*deegas con tom*at*-eh	
banderillas	savouries on sticks
bander*ee*-yas	
berberechos	cockles in vinegar
bairbehr*ech*-os	
callos	tripe, usually in hot paprika sauce
c*a*-yos	
caracoles	snails
carracol-es	

empanadillas	small pastries with a variety of
empannade*ee*-yas	fillings
patatas bravas	fried potatoes in spicy sauce
pat*a*t-as br*a*b-as	
pimientos rellenos	stuffed peppers
pim-yentos rel-yenos	
pinchitos	grilled kidneys or spicy sausages
pinch*ee*tos	(usually on skewers)
tortilla de patata	Spanish omelet, made of
tort*ee*-ya deh pat*a*t-ah	potatoes and onions

[For other essential expressions see 'Ordering a drink', p. 80]

In a restaurant

ESSENTIAL INFORMATION

- The place to ask for: **un restaurante** [*see p. 17*]
- You can eat at these places:
  RESTAURANTE
  CAFETERIA (luxurious café)
  HOSTERIA
  MESON
  PARADOR } (regional cooking)
  POSADA
  ALBERGUE DE CARRETERA (roadside inn)
  FONDA (cheap simple food)
  MERENDERO (on the outskirts of a town suitable for meals or snacks during the early evening)
  CASA DE COMIDAS (a simple restaurant with typical Spanish food)
- You may also find **CASA** plus the name of the owner.
- Tipping is very common in Spain and it is usual to leave 10% of the bill for the waiter.
- By law, the menus must be displayed outside or in the window and that is the only way to judge if a place is right for your needs.
- Self-service restaurants (**AUTOSERVICIO**) are not unknown, but all other places have waiter service.
- Restaurants are usually open from 1 p.m. – 3/3.30 p.m. and from 9 p.m. – 11.30 p.m. but this can vary. It's not difficult to get a meal before 9 p.m. because lots of restaurants, especially **CASAS DE COMIDAS** or **MESONES** provide meals in the early evening (**meriendas**). And if you want to eat before 1 p.m. you can always try some **tapas** which can be a meal in themselves.
- By law, **Hojas de Reclamaciones** (Complaints Forms) must be kept in restaurants as well as in hotels, bars and petrol stations. All complaints are investigated by the Tourist Authority.

WHAT TO SAY

May I book a table?	**¿Puedo reservar una mesa?**
	pwed-o res-airbar oona mes-ah
I've booked a table	**He reservado una mesa**
	eh res-airbad-o oona mes-ah
A table ...	**Una mesa ...**
	oona mes-ah ...
for one	**para uno**
	para oono
for three	**para tres**
	para tres
The à la carte menu, please	**El menú a la carta, por favor**
	el menoo ah la carta por fab-or
The fixed-price menu	**El menú de precio fijo**
	el menoo deh preth-yo fee-ho
The (300) pesetas menu	**El menú de (trescientas) pesetas**
	el menoo deh (tres-thee-entas) pes-et-as
The tourist menu	**El menú turistico**
	el menoo touristico
Today's special menu	**El menú del día**
	el menoo del deea
The wine list	**La lista de vinos**
	la leesta deh beenos
What's this, please? [*point to menu*]	**¿Qué es eso, por favor?**
	keh es es-o por fab-or
A carafe of wine, please	**Una jarra de vino, por favor**
	oona harra deh beeno por fab-or
A quarter (25cc)	**Un cuarto**
	oon cwarto
A half (50cc)	**Medio**
	med-yo
A glass	**Un vaso**
	oon basso
A bottle	**Una botella**
	oona botel-ya
A half-bottle	**Media botella**
	med-ya botel-ya
A litre	**Un litro**
	oon litro

Red/white/rosé/house wine	**Tinto/blanco/rosado/vino de la casa** t*i*nto/blanco/rosad-o/*bee*no deh la c*a*s-ah
Some more bread, please	**Mas pan, por favor** mas pan por fab-*o*r
Some more wine	**Mas vino** mas b*ee*no
Some oil	**Aceite** ath*a*y-teh
Some vinegar	**Vinagre** been*a*g-reh
Some salt/some pepper	**Sal/pimienta** s*a*l/pim-y*e*nta
Some water	**Agua** *a*gwa
With/without garlic	**Sin/con ajo** sin/con *a*ho
How much does that come to?	**¿Cuánto es?** cw*a*nto es
Is service included?	**¿Está incluído el servicio?** est*a* incloo-*ee*do el sairb*i*th-yo
Where is the toilet, please?	**¿Dónde está el servicio, por favor?** d*o*ndeh est*a* el sairb*i*th-yo por fab-*o*r
Miss! [*This does not sound abrupt in Spanish*]	**¡Señorita!** sen-yor*ee*ta
Waiter!	**¡Camarero!** camma-r*ai*ro
The bill, please	**La cuenta, por favor** la cw*e*nta por fab-*o*r

Key words for courses, as seen on some menus:
[*Only ask this question if you want the waiter to remind you of the choice.*]

What have you got in the way of ...	**¿Qué tienen de ...** keh tee-*e*n-en deh ...
STARTERS?	**ENTREMESES?** entreh-m*e*ss-es
SOUP	**SOPAS?** s*o*pas

EGG DISHES?	**HUEVOS?**
	web-os
FISH?	**PESCADOS?**
	pescad-os
MEAT?	**CARNES?**
	carnes
GAME?	**CAZA?**
	catha
FOWL?	**AVES?**
	abes
VEGETABLES?	**VERDURAS/LEGUMBRES?**
	bairdoo-ras/leh-goom-bres
CHEESE?	**QUESOS?**
	kes-os
FRUIT?	**FRUTAS?**
	frootas
ICE-CREAM?	**HELADOS?**
	eladdos
DESSERT?	**POSTRES?**
	pos-tres

UNDERSTANDING THE MENU

- You will find the names of the principal ingredients of most dishes on these pages:

  Starters p. 69   Fruit p. 71
  Meat p. 74   Cheese p. 70
  Fish p. 78   Ice-cream p. 63
  Vegetables p. 72   Dessert p. 61

- Used together with the following lists of cooking and menu terms, they should help you to decode the menu.
- These cooking and menu terms are for understanding only, not for speaking aloud.

Cooking and menu terms

con aceite	in oil
en adobo	marinated in red wine
al ajillo	in garlic sauce
con ajolio (allioli)	in garlic mayonnaise

ahumado	smoked
en almíbar	in syrup
asado (al ast)	roasted
a la barbacoa	barbecued
a la brasa	grilled on an open fire
en cacerola	casserole
caldo	stock
caliente	hot
cocido	boiled
crudo	raw
a la chilindrón	with tomatoes, peppers and onion
dulce	sweet
en dulce	in sweet sauce
duro	hard boiled
empanado	fried in breadcrumbs
en escabeche	marinated
escalfado	poached
estofado	braised/stewed
flameado	flamed
a la francesa	with milk, flour and butter
frio	cold
frito	fried
gratinado	browned with breadcrumbs or cheese
guisado	stewed
hervido	boiled
horneado	baked
al horno	baked
al jerez	in sherry
en su jugo	pot roasted
con mantequilla	with butter
marinado (a la marinera)	marinated
al minuto	prepared in a very short time
a la parrilla	grilled
pasado por agua	soft boiled
con perejil	with parsley
a la pescadora	with egg, lemon, wine and vinegar
a la plancha	grilled
rehogado	fried in oil with garlic and vinegar
relleno	stuffed
a la romana	deep fried
salado	salted

en salazón	cured
en salsa	in a sauce
en salsa blanca	in a white sauce
salsa mahonesa	in a mayonnaise sauce
salsa verde	sauce made from white wine, herbs, onion and flour
salsa vinagreta	sauce made from salt, vinegar and oil
salteado	sautéed
tostado	toasted
trufado	stuffed with truffles
al vapor	steamed
a la vasca	with asparagus, peas, egg, herbs, garlic, onion and flour
en vinagre	in vinegar

Further words to help you understand the menu:

anguilas	eels
arroz a la cubana	rice, fried eggs, bananas and tomato sauce
arroz a la milanesa	rice with 'chorizo' (spicy sausage), ham, cheese and peas
atún	tuna
brazo de gitano	cake filled with cream or marmalade
buñuelos (buñuelitos)	small fritters with a variety of fillings
cabeza (de cordero)	lamb's head
caldereta	fish or lamb stew
callos (a la madrileña)	tripe in piquant sauce
cocido (madrileño)	vegetable and meat stew with beans or chick-peas
codorniz	quail
cochinillo asado	suckling pig, roasted
congrio	conger eel
conejo a la aragonesa	rabbit cooked with onion, garlic, almonds and herbs
consomé	clear soup
criadillas	sweetbreads
cuajada	coagulated milk, similar to yogurt

empanada gallega	tenderloin of pork, onions and chilli pepper as filling
fabada	beans, black pudding, ham, pig's ear, onion and garlic in a stew
flan	cream caramel
gallina en pepitoria	chicken casserole with almonds and saffron
ganso	goose
garbanzos	chick-peas
gazpacho	cold spicy soup made of onion, tomatoes, peppers, bread, garlic, oil and vinegar
huevos a la flamenca	eggs baked with tomato, ham, onion, asparagus and peppers
huevos al plato	fried eggs
huevos revueltos	scrambled eggs
lentejas	lentils
lengua aragonesa	tongue with vegetables
liebre	hare
lomo	loin
magras con tomate	smoked ham fried with tomatoes
menestra (de verduras, de carne o pollo)	mixed vegetable, or meat, or chicken stew
mero (lubina)	sea bass
migas	bits of bread fried with garlic, spicy sausages, bacon and ham
natillas	custard
paella catalana	spicy pork sausages, pork, squid, tomato, chilli pepper and peas
paella marinera	fish and seafood only
paella valenciana	the classic paella with chicken, mussels, shrimp, prawns, peas, tomato, peppers and garlic
parrillada	boned and shelled fish, shellfish, chicken and meat, fried
pastel de carne	meat pie
pato	duck
pavo	turkey
perdiz	partridge
pimientos a la riojana	sweet peppers stuffed with minced meat
pisto	fried mixed vegetables

pollo a la chilindrón	chicken fried with tomatoes, peppers and smoked ham **or** bacon
potaje	vegetable stew
pote gallego	beans, meat, potatoes and cabbage
puchero de gallina	stewed chicken
salmonete	red mullet
sesos	brains (of lamb)
solomillo	tenderloin steak (of pork)
sopa Juliana	shredded vegetable soup
ternasco a la aragonesa	young lamb roasted with potatoes and garlic
tocino	bacon
toro de lidia	beef from the bullring
torrijas	bread soaked in milk and egg and then fried, sprinkled with sugar (french toast)
tortilla francesa	plain omelet
tortilla de patatas/española	typical Spanish omelet made with potatoes
trucha a la navarra	trout filled with smoked ham
zarzuela	savoury stew of assorted fish and shellfish

Health

ESSENTIAL INFORMATION

- For details of reciprocal health agreements between your country and the country you are visiting, visit your local Department of Health office at least one month before leaving, or ask your travel agent.
- Take your own 'first line' first aid kit with you.
- For minor disorders and treatment at a drug store, see p. 40.
- For finding your way to a doctor, dentist or drug store, see p. 17.
- In case of sudden illiness or an accident, you can go to a **CASA DE SOCORRO.** These are emergency first aid centres open to the general public and are free. If you have a serious accident, the same free service is provided by an **equipo quirurgico.** If you are on the road there are **PUESTOS DE SOCORRO** (first aid centres) run by the **CRUZ ROJA** (Red Cross).
- It's sometimes difficult to get an ambulance. In an emergency you are legally entitled to drive at speed, sounding your horn and waving a white handkerchief, to the nearest hospital or first aid centre: other vehicles are required by law to give way to you. If you do not have a car, wave down a motorist.
- Once in the country, decide a definite plan of action in case of serious illness: communicate your problem to a near neighbour, the receptionist or someone you see regularly. You are then dependent on that person helping you obtain treatment.
- To find a doctor in an emergency, look for:
  Médicos (in the Yellow Pages of the telephone directory)
  Urgencias (Casualty department)
  Casas de Socorro
  Puestos de Socorro ⎤ (First aid centres)
  H
  Hospital ⎤ (Hospital)

What's the matter?

I have a pain in my ...

Me duele ...
meh dwel-eh ...

abdomen	**el abdomen** el abdomen
ankle	**el tobillo** el tobee-yo
arm	**el brazo** el brath-o
back	**la espalda** la espalda
bladder	**la vejiga** la behee-ga
bowels	**el vientre** el bee-entreh
breast/chest	**el pecho** el pech-o
ear	**el oído** el oy-eedo
eye	**el ojo** el o-ho
foot	**el pie** el pee-eh
head	**la cabeza** la cabbeth-ah
heel	**el talón** el talon
jaw	**la mandíbula** la mandiboola
kidney	**el riñon** el rin-yon
leg	**la pierna** la pee-airna
lung	**el pulmón** el poolmon
neck	**el cuello** el cwel-yo
penis	**el pene** el pen-eh
shoulder	**el hombro** el ombro
stomach	**el estómago** el estommago

I have a pain in my . . .	**Me duele . . .** meh dwel-eh . . .
testicle	**el testículo** el testicoolo
throat	**la garganta** la garganta
vagina	**la vagina** la ba-heena
wrist	**la muñeca** la moon-yek-ah
I have a pain here [point]	**Me duele aquí** meh dwel-eh ak-ee
I have a toothache	**Me duelen las muelas** meh dwel-en las mwel-as
I have broken . . .	**Me he roto . . .** meh eh rot-o . . .
my dentures	**la dentadura** la dentadoora
my glasses	**las gafas** las gaf-as
I have lost . . .	**He perdido . . .** eh pairdeedo . . .
my contact lenses	**mis lentes de contacto** mees lent-es deh contacto
a filling	**un empaste** oon empasteh
My child is ill	**Mi hijo/a está enfermo a*** mee eeho/ah esta enfairmo/ah
He/she has a pain in his/her . . . ankle [see list above]	**Le duele . . .** leh dwel-eh . . . **el tobillo** el tobee-yo
How bad is it?	
I'm ill	**Estoy enfermo/a*** estoy enfairmo/ah
It's urgent	**Es urgente** es oor-henteh
It's serious	**Es grave** es grab-eh
It's not serious	**No es grave** no es grab-eh

* For boys use 'o', for girls use 'a'.

It hurts	**Me duele**
	meh dwel-eh
It hurts a lot	**Me duele mucho**
	meh dwel-eh moocho
It doesn't hurt much	**No me duele mucho**
	no meh dwel-eh moocho
The pain occurs ...	**El dolor ocurre ...**
	el dol-or ocoo-reh ...
every quarter of an hour	**cada cuarto de hora**
	cad-ah cwarto deh ora
every half hour	**cada media hora**
	cad-ah med-ya ora
every hour	**cada hora**
	cad-ah ora
every day	**cada día**
	cad-ah deea
It hurts most of the time	**Me duele casi todo el tiempo**
	meh dwel-eh cas-ee tod-o el
	tee-empo
I've had it for ...	**Lo tengo desde hace ...**
	lo tengo desdeh ath-eh ...
one hour/one day	**una hora/un día**
	oona ora/oon deea
two hours/two days	**dos horas/dos días**
	dos oras/dos deeas
It's a ...	**Es un ...**
	es oon ...
sharp pain	**dolor agudo**
	dol-or agoodo
dull ache	**dolor sordo**
	dol-or sordo
nagging pain	**dolor continuo**
	dol-or contin-wo
I feel ...	**Me siento ...**
	meh see-ento ...
dizzy	**mareado**
	marreh-ad-o
sick	**mareado (con nauseas)**
	marreh-ad-o (con nows-yas)
weak	**débil**
	deb-eel
feverish	**con fiebre**
	con fee-eb-reh

Already under treatment for something else?

I take . . . regularly [*show*]	**Tomo . . . regularmente**
	tom-o . . . regoolarmenteh
this medicine	**esta medicina**
	*e*sta medith*ee*na
these pills	**estas píldoras**
	*e*stas p*i*ldor-**as**
I have . . .	**Tengo . . .**
	t*e*ngo . . .
haemorrhoids	**hemorroides**
	emmoro-*ee*d-**es**
rheumatism	**reuma**
	reh-*oo*ma
I am . . .	**Soy . . .**
	s*oy* . . .
diabetic	**diabético/a***
	dee-ab*e*t-eeco/ah
asthmatic	**asmático/a***
	asm*a*tico/ah
I am allergic to (penicillin)	**Soy alérgico/a a (la penicilina)***
	s*oy* al*air*-heeco/ah ah (la penni-thil*ee*na)
I am pregnant	**Estoy embarazada**
	est*oy* embarrath*a*d-ah
I have a heart condition	**Estoy del corazón**
	est*oy* del corath*o*n

Other essential expressions

Please can you help?	**Por favor, ¿puede ayudar?**
	por fab-*or* pwed-eh a-yood*a*r
A doctor, please	**Un doctor, por favor**
	un doct*o*r por fab-*or*
A dentist	**Un dentista**
	oon dent*i*sta
I don't speak Spanish	**No hablo español**
	no *a*blo espan-y*o*l

* Men use 'o', women use 'a'.

What time does ... arrive?	¿A qué hora llega ...
	ah keh ora yeg-ah ...
the doctor	el doctor?
	el doctor
the dentist	el dentista?
	el dentista

From the doctor: key sentences to understand

Take this ...	Tome esto ...
	tom-eh esto ...
every day	cada día
	cad-ah deea
every hour	cada hora
	cad-ah ora
twice/four times a day	dos/cuatro veces al día
	dos/cwatro beth-es al deea
Stay in bed	Guarde cama
	gwar-deh cama
Don't travel	No viaje
	no bee-ah-heh
for ... days/weeks	hasta dentro de ... días/semanas
	asta dentro deh ...
	deeas/sem-annas
You must go to hospital	Tiene que ir al hospital
	tee-en-eh keh eer al ospital

Problems: complaints, loss, theft

ESSENTIAL INFORMATION

- Problems with
  camping facilities, see p. 34   health, see p. 94
  household appliances, see p. 52   the car, see p. 110
- If the worst comes to the worst, find the police station. To ask the way, see p. 17
- Look for:
  COMISARIA DE POLICIA (police station)
  CUARTEL DE LA GUARDIA CIVIL
  (Civil Guard — in small towns and villages)
  OFICINA DE OBJETOS PERDIDOS (lost property office)
- If you lose your passport, go to your nearest Consulate.
- In an emergency dial 091 for the police. The numbers for Fire and Ambulance differ according to region. Remember, however, that the ambulance service is not free and nor are emergency calls from public phones.

COMPLAINTS

I bought this ...	**Compré esto ...**
	compr*eh* esto ...
today	**hoy**
	oy
yesterday	**ayer**
	a-y*air*
on Monday [*see p.135*]	**el lunes**
	el *loon*-es
It's no good	**No está bien**
	no est*a* bee-*en*
Look	**Mire**
	mee-r*eh*
Here [*point*]	**Aquí**
	ak-*ee*
Can you ...	**¿Puede ...**
	pw*ed*-eh ...
change it?	**cambiarlo?**
	camb-y*a*rlo

give me a refund?	**devolverme el dinero?**
	debolb*air*meh el din-*airo*
mend it?	**arreglarlo?**
	arreglar-lo
Here's the receipt	**Aquí está el recibo**
	ak-*ee* esta el ret*hee*bo
Can I see the manager?	**¿Puedo ver al director?**
	pwed-o b*air* al dir*rect*or

LOSS

[See also 'Theft' below; the lists are interchangeable]

I have lost ...	**He perdido ...**
	eh pair*deedo* ...
my bag	**mi bolso**
	mee *bolso*
my bracelet	**mi pulsera**
	mee pools*aira*
my camera	**mi cámara**
	mee *camara*
my car keys	**las llaves de mi coche**
	las *yab*-es deh mee coch-eh
my car logbook	**mi cartilla de propriedad**
	mee car*tee*-ya deh prop-yed-*ad*
my driving licence	**mi carnet de conducir**
	mee carnet deh condoo*theer*
my insurance certificate	**mi certificado del seguro**
	mee thair-tificad-o del seg*oo*-ro
my jewellery	**mi joyas**
	mees *hoy*-as
everything	**todo**
	tod-o

THEFT

[See also 'Loss' above; the lists are interchangeable]

Someone has stolen ...	**Alguien ha robado ...**
	alg-yen ah robbad-o ...
my car	**mi coche**
	mee *coch*-eh
my car radio	**la radio de mi coche**
	la rad-yo deh mee *coch*-eh

Someone has stolen ... **Alguien ha robado ...**
*a*lg-yen ah robb*a*d-o ...

my keys mis llaves
mees y*a*b-es

my money mi dinero
mee din-*air*o

my necklace mi collar
mee col-y*ar*

my passport mi pasaporte
mee pas-a-p*o*rteh

my radio mi radio
mee r*a*d-yo

my tickets mis billetes
mees bee-yet-es

my travellers' cheques mis cheques de viaje
mees check-es deh bee-*a*h-heh

my wallet mi cartera
mee c*a*rt*air*a

my watch mi reloj
mee rel-*o*k

my luggage mi equipaje
mee ek-eep*a*-heh

LIKELY REACTIONS: key words to understand

Wait **Espere**
esp*air*-eh

When? **¿Cuándo?**
cw*a*ndo

Where? **¿Dónde?**
d*o*ndeh

Name? **¿Nombre?**
n*o*mbreh

Address? **¿Dirección?**
dirrekth-y*o*n

I can't help you? **No puedo ayudarle**
no pwed-o a-yood*a*rleh

Nothing to do with me **Yo no tengo nada que ver**
*y*o no tengo n*a*d-ah keh b*air*

The post office

ESSENTIAL INFORMATION

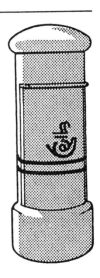

- To find a post office, see p. 17.
- Key words to look for:
  CORREOS
  CORREOS Y TELEGRAFOS
  SERVICIO POSTAL
- For stamps look for the words:
  SELLOS or **TIMBRES**
  or **FRANQUEOS**
- It is best to buy stamps at the smoke shop. Only go to the post office for more complicated transactions, like telegrams.
- Look for this red and yellow sign on the shop:
- Letter boxes **(buzones)** are yellow. Post all overseas mail in the opening marked **EXTRANJERO.**
- For poste restante you should show your passport at the counter marked **LISTA DE CORREOS** in the main post office. A small fee will be charged.

WHAT TO SAY

To England, please   **Para Inglaterra, por favor**
para íngla-terra por fab-*or*

[Hand letters, cards or parcels over the counter]

To Australia   **Para Australia**
para ah-oostral-ya

To the United States   **Para los Estados Unidos**
para los estad-os oon*ee*dos

[For other countries, see p. 138]

How much is . . .   ¿**Cuánto es . . .**
                        cwanto es . . .

  this parcel (to Canada)?   **este paquete (para Canadá)?**
                                       este pak*e*t-eh (p*a*ra canad*a*)

  a letter (to Australia)?   **una carta (para Australia)?**
                                      *oo*na c*a*rta (p*a*ra ah-oostr*a*l-ya)

  a postcard (to England)?   **una postal (para Inglaterra)?**
                                      *oo*na post*a*l (p*a*ra ingla-te*rr*a)

Airmail   **Por avión**
              por ab-y*o*n

Surface mail   **Por correo ordinario**
                   por cor-r*e*h-o ordin*a*ree-o

One stamp, please   **Un sello, por favor**
                        oon s*e*l-yo por fab-*o*r

Two stamps   **Dos sellos**
                 dos s*e*l-yos

One (15 pts) stamp   **Un sello (de quince pesetas)**
                         oon s*e*l-yo (deh k*i*ntheh pes-*e*t-as)

I'd like to send a telegram   **Quiero enviar un telegrama**
                                  kee-*air*o embee-*a*r oon
                                    telegr*a*mma

Telephoning

ESSENTIAL INFORMATION

- Public telephones (**cabinas telefónicas**) are metallic grey with the words **TELEFONOS** on a green background. Calls abroad can only be made from boxes marked **INTERNACIONAL.**
- To ask the way to a public telephone, see p. 17.
- To use a public telephone: insert a 50 pts coin in the slot, lift the receiver, wait for dial tone, dial 07, wait for higher tone, dial country code (UK – 44; USA – 1; Australia – 61) then dial the town/area code followed by the subscriber's number. The following coins can be used to prolong the call: 5 pts, 25 pts, 50 pts.
- To make a phone call from a café, you will have to buy a **ficha** (counter). These are sold in cafés and are used in place of coins.
- For calls to countries which cannot be dialled direct or if you have difficulties in placing a call, go to the **CENTRAL TELEFONICA (CTNE)** or **TELEFONOS** which in large towns are open twenty-four hours a day. In **la Telefonica,** the operator will put your call through and give you the bill afterwards. Just write the town and number you want on a piece of paper and hand it over to the operator. Add **de persona a persona** if you want a person-to-person call or **a cobro revertido** if you want to reverse the charges.
- In Spain the telephone network operates independently of the post office, so don't expect to find phones in post offices.

WHAT TO SAY

Where can I make a telephone call?	**¿Dónde puedo llamar por teléfono?**
	dondeh pwed-o yamar por telef-ono
Local/abroad	**Local/al extranjero**
	local/ al extran-hairo

I'd like this number ...
   [*show number*]
   in England

   in Canada

   in the USA

Quiero este número ...
kee-*airo* esteh n*oo*mairo ...
en Inglaterra
en ingla-*terra*
en Canadá
en canad*a*
en los Estados Unidos
en los est*a*d-os ooneed*o*s

[*For other countries, see p. 138*]

Can you dial it for me,
   please?

**¿Puede usted marcar por mí, por
   favor?**
pw*e*d-eh oosted marc*a*r por m*ee*
   por fab-*o*r

How much is it?

¿Cuánto es?
cw*a*nto *e*s

Hello!

¡Hola!
o-la

May I speak to ... ?

¿Puedo hablar con ... ?
pw*e*d-o abl*a*r con ...

Extension

Extensión
extens-y*o*n

I'm sorry, I don't speak
   Spanish

Lo siento, no hablo español
lo see-*e*nto no *a*blo espan-y*o*l

Do you speak English?

¿Habla usted inglés?
*a*bla oosted in-gl*e*s

Thank you, I'll phone back

Gracias, volveré a llamar
grath-yas bolbair-eh ah yam*a*r

Good-bye

Adiós
ad-y*o*s

LIKELY REACTIONS

That's 80 pesetas	**Son ochenta pesetas** son ochenta pes-*et*-as
Cabin number (3)	**Cabina número (tres)** cabeena n*oo*mairo tres

[*For numbers, see p. 131*]

Don't hang up	**No cuelgue** no cw*el*g-eh
I'm trying to connect you	**Estoy intentando comunicarle** est*oy* intent*a*ndo comoonic*a*rleh
You're through	**Hable** *a*b-leh
There's a delay	**Hay retraso** *a*h-ee retr*a*s-o
I'll try again	**Probaré otra vez** proba-*reh ot*-ra beth

Changing checks and money

ESSENTIAL INFORMATION

- Finding your way to a bank or change bureau, see p. 17.
- Look for these words:
  BANCO (bank)
  CAJA DE AHORROS (savings bank)
  CAMBIO (change)
  CAJA DE CAMBIO (cash desk in a bank)
  OFICINA DE CAMBIO (bureau de change)
- To cash your normal checks, exactly as at home, use your banker's card where you see the Eurocheque sign. Write in English.
- Have your passport handy and remember that in Spain banks open at 9 a.m. and close at 2 p.m. and on Saturdays at 1 p.m.

WHAT TO SAY

I'd like to cash ...

Quiero cobrar ...
kee-*airo* cobr*ar* ...

  this travellers' cheque

este cheque de viaje
esteh check-eh deh bee-*ah*-heh

  these travellers' cheques

estos cheques de viaje
estos check-es deh bee-*ah*-heh

  this cheque

este cheque
esteh check-eh

I'd like to change this into Spanish pesetas

Quiero cambiar esto en pesetas españolas
kee-*airo* camb-y*ar* esto en pes-*et*-as espan-*yolas*

Here's ...

Aquí está ...
ak-*ee* esta ...

  my banker's card

mi tarjeta de banco
mee tarh*et*-ah deh b*anco*

  my passport

mi pasaporte
mee pas-ap*orteh*

For excursions into neighbouring countries:

I'd like to change this ...	**Quiero cambiar esto ...**
[*show banknotes*]	kee-*airo* camb-y*ar* esto ...
into French francs	**en francos franceses**
	en fr*anc*-os franth*es*-es
into Italian lire	**en liras italianas**
	en l*ee*-ras itali*a*nnas
into Portuguese escudos	**en escudos portugueses**
	en esc*oo*dos portoog*es*-es
What is the rate of exchange?	**¿A cuánto está el cambio?**
	ah cw*a*nto est*a* el c*a*mb-yo

LIKELY REACTIONS

Passport, please	**Pasaporte, por favor**
	pas-ap*or*teh por fab-*or*
Sign here	**Firme aquí**
	f*ee*r-meh ak-*ee*
Your banker's card, please	**Su tarjeta de banco, por favor**
	soo tarhet-ah deh b*a*nco por fab-*or*
Go to the cash desk	**Vaya a caja**
	b*a*-ya ah c*a*-ha

Car travel

ESSENTIAL INFORMATION

- Finding a filling station or garage, see p. 17.
- Look for these signs:
  GASOLINA (gasoline)
  GASOLINERA (gas station)
  ESTACION DE SERVICIO (gas station)
- Grades of gasoline: **EXTRA** (4 star)
  NORMAL (2 star standard) **GAS-OIL** (diesel)
  SUPER (3 star) **DOS TIEMPOS** (two stroke)
- 1 gallon is about 4½ liters (accurate enough up to 6 gallons).
- Petrol prices are standardized all over Spain, and a minimum sale of 5 liters is often imposed.
- For car repairs, look for signs with red, blue and white stripes or
  GARAJE
  TALLER DE REPARACIONES
- Most gas stations operate a 24-hour service, though some close late at night. Take care, however, as the stations themselves are few and far between.
- Garages will open at 8 or 9 a.m. and close between 7:30 and 8 p.m. Most will close lunchtime.
- Unfamiliar road signs and warnings, see p. 125.

WHAT TO SAY

[*For numbers, see p. 131*]

(Nine) litres of ...	(Nueve) litros de ...
	(nw*e*b-eh) l*i*tros deh ...
(Five hundred) pesetas of ...	(Quinientas) pesetas de ...
	(kin-yentas) pes-*et*-as deh ...
standard	**normal**
	norm*a*l
premium	**super**
	s*oo*pair
diesel	**gas-oil**
	gas-*oi*l
Fill it up, please	**Lleno, por favor**
	y*e*no por fab-*or*

Can you check ...
¿Puede mirar ...
pwed-eh mee-rar ...

the oil?
el aceite?
el athay-teh

the battery?
la batería?
la batteh-reea

the radiator?
el radiador?
el rad-yad-or

the tyres?
los neumáticos?
los neh-oomatticos

I've run out of petrol
Me he quedado sin gasolina
meh eh ked-ad-o sin gasoleena

Can I borrow a can, please?
¿Puede dejarme una lata, por favor?
pwed-eh deh-harmeh oona latta por fab-or

My car has broken down
Se ha averiado mi coche
se ah abbeh-ree-ado mee coch-eh

My car won't start
Mi coche no arranca
mee coch-eh no arranca

I've had an accident
He tenido un accidente
eh teneedo oon ak-theedenteh

I've lost my car keys
He perdido las llaves de mi coche
eh pairdeedo las yab-es deh mee coch-eh

My car is ...
Mi coche está ...
mee coch-eh esta ...

two kilometres away
a dos kilómetros
ah dos kilometros

three kilometres away
a tres kilómetros
ah tres kilometros

Can you help me, please?
¿Puede ayudarme, por favor
pwed-eh a-yoodarmeh por fab-or

Do you do repairs?
¿Hacen reparaciones?
ath-en reparath-yon-es

I have a puncture
Tengo un neumático pinchado
tengo oon neh-oomattico pinchad-o

I have a broken windscreen
Tengo el parabrisas roto
tengo el parabrees-as rot-o

I think the problem is here ... [point]
Creo que el problema esta aquí ...
creh-o keh el problem-ah esta ak-ee ...

I don't know what's wrong
No se lo que está mal
no seh lo keh esta mal

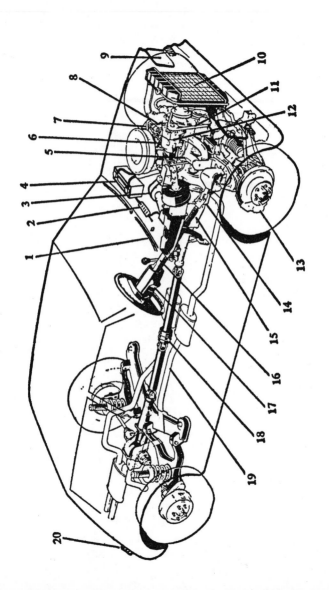

English	Spanish	Pronunciation
1 windscreen wipers	limpiaparabrisas	limp-ya-parabree-sas
2 fuses	fusibles	fooseebles
3 heater	calentador	calenta-dor
4 battery	batería	batteh-reea
5 engine	motor	mot-or
6 fuel pump	bomba de gasolina	bomba deh gasoleena
7 starter motor	motor de arranque	mot-or deh arrankeh
8 carburettor	carburador	carboo-rãd-or
9 lights	faros	faros
10 radiator	radiador	rad-yad-or
11 fan belt	correa del ventilador	correh-ah del bentillador
12 generator	generador	henneh-rad-or
13 brakes	frenos	fren-os
14 clutch	embrague	embrag-eh
15 gear box	caja de cambios	ca-ha de camb-yos
16 steering	dirección	dirrekth-yon
17 ignition	encendido	enthendeedo
18 transmission	transmisión	transmis-yon
19 exhaust	tubo de escape	toobo deh escap-eh
20 indicators	indicadores	indic-ad-or-es

Can you . . .	**¿Puede . . .** pwed-eh . . .
repair the fault?	**reparar la avería?** repparar la abbeh-reea
come and look?	**venir a ver?** ben-eer ah bair
estimate the cost?	**estimar el coste?** estimar el costeh
write it down?	**escribirlo?** escrib-eer-lo
Do you accept these coupons?	**¿Aceptan estos cupones?** atheptan estos coopon-es
How long will the repair take?	**¿Cuánto tiempo tardarán en repararlo?** cwanto tee-empo tarda-ran en reppar-ar-lo
When will the car be ready?	**¿Cuando estará listo el coche?** cwando estara listo el coch-eh
Can I see the bill?	**¿Puedo ver la cuenta?** pwed-o bair la cwenta
This is my insurance document	**Este es mi documento del seguro** esteh es mee docoomento del segoo-ro

HIRING A CAR

Can I hire a car?	**¿Puedo alquilar un coche?** pwed-o alkeelar oon coch-eh
I need a car . . .	**Necesito un coche . . .** neth-eseeto oon coch-eh . . .
for two people	**para dos personas** para dos pairson-as
for five people	**para cinco personas** para thinko pairson-as
for one day	**para un día** para oon deea
for five days	**para cinco días** para thinko deeas
for a week	**para una semana** para oona sem-anna

Can you write down ...	¿Puede escribir ... pwed-eh escrib-eer ...
the deposit to pay?	el depósito de pago? el deposit-o deh pag-o
the charge per kilometre?	el precio por kilómetro? el preth-yo por kilometro
the daily charge?	el precio por día? el preth-yo por deea
the cost of insurance?	el precio del seguro? el preth-yo del segoo-ro
Can I leave it in (Madrid)?	¿Puedo dejarlo en (Madrid) pwed-o deh-harlo en (madrid)
What documents do I need?	¿Que documentos necesito? keh docoomentos neth-eseeto

LIKELY REACTIONS

We don't do repairs	No se hacen reparaciones no seh ath-en reparath-yon-es
Where is your car?	¿Dónde está su coche? dondeh esta soo coch-eh
What make is it?	¿Qué tipo es? keh teepo es
Come back tomorrow/on Monday	Vuelva mañana/el lunes bwelba manyan-ah/el loon-es

[For days of the week, see p. 135]

We don't hire cars	No se alquilan coches no seh alkeelan coch-es
Your driving licence, please	Su carnet de conducir, por favor soo carnet deh condoo-theer por fab-or
The mileage is unlimited	El kilometraje es ilimitado el kilometra-heh es illimit-ad-o

Public transport

ESSENTIAL INFORMATION

- Finding the way to a bus station, bus stop, trolley stop, railway station and taxi-stand, see p. 17.
- Taxis are usually black sedans with a coloured line painted along the side. They display a green light at night and during the day a sign on the windshield which says **LIBRE** (free) if they are available.
- These are the different types of trains, graded according to speed (slowest to fastest):

  TAF/FERROBUS/OMNIBUS
  TRANVIAS/AUTOMOTOR (all short distance local trains, not very reliable)
  EXPRESO/RAPIDO (do not be misled by their names; these are both *slow* trains the only difference being the first travels by night, the second by day)
  ELECTROTREN (fast and comfortable)
  TER (fast and comfortable – supplement payable)
  TALGO (luxury train – supplement payable)
- Key words on signs [*see also p. 125*]
  ANDEN (platform)
  BILLETES (tickets, ticket office)
  CONSIGNA/EQUIPAJES (left-luggage)
  DESPACHO DE BILLETES/TAQUILLA (ticket office)
  ENTRADA (entrance)
  HORARIO (timetable)
  LLEGADA (arrival)
  OFICINA DE INFORMACION (information office)
  PARADA (bus stop, taxi stop)
  PROHIBIDO (forbidden)
  RENFE (initials of Spanish railways)
  SALIDA (exit)
- Children travel free up to the age of three and pay half-price up to the age of seven. However, if you have an international ticket, children can travel free up to the age of four and travel half-price up to the age of twelve.
- On certain dates throughout the year known as **Días Azules** (Blue Days), numerous reductions are available on train travel;

check with the Spanish Tourist Office for dates and further information.
- On buses and tubes there is a flat rate irrespective of distance and it is cheaper to buy a taco (book of tickets) for underground travel. Tubes operate between 6 a.m. and 1 a.m.
- It is worth booking train and coach journeys in advance.

WHAT TO SAY

Where does the train for (Madrid) leave from?	**¿De dónde sale el tren para (Madrid)?** deh dondeh sal-eh el tren para (madrid)
At what time does the train leave for (Madrid)?	**¿A qué hora sale el tren para (Madrid)?** ah keh ora sal-eh el tren para (madrid)
At what time does the train arrive in (Madrid)?	**¿A qué hora llega el tren a (Madrid)?** ah keh ora yeg-ah el tren ah (madrid)
Is this the train for (Madrid)?	**¿Es éste el tren para (Madrid)?** es esteh el tren para (madrid)
Where does the bus for (Barcelona) leave from?	**¿De dónde sale el autobús para (Barcelona)?** deh dondeh sal-eh el ah-ooto-boos para (barthelona)
At what time does the bus leave for (Barcelona)?	**¿A qué hora sale el autobús para (Barcelona)?** ah keh ora sal-eh el ah-ooto-boos para (barthelona)
At what times does the bus arrive at (Barcelona)?	**¿A qué hora llega el autobús a (Barcelona)?** ah keh ora yeg-ah el ah-ooto-boos a (barthelona)
Is this the bus for (Barcelona)?	**¿Es éste el autobús para (Barcelona)?** es esteh el ah-ooto-boos para (barthelona)
Do I have to change?	**¿Tengo que cambiar?** tengo keh camb-yar

Where does ... leave from?	**¿De dónde sale ...**
	deh dondeh sal-eh ...
the bus	**el autobús**
	el ah-ooto-boos
the boat/ferry	**el barco/ferry**
	el barco/ferree
the train	**el tren**
	el tren
the underground	**el metro**
	el metro
for the airport	**para el aeropuerto?**
	para el airo-pwairto
for the cathedral	**para la catedral?**
	para la cattedral
for the beach	**para la playa?**
	para la pla-ya
for the market place	**para el mercado?**
	para el maircad-o
for the railway station	**para la estación de tren?**
	para la estath-yon deh tren
for the town centre	**para el centro de la ciudad?**
	para el thentro deh la thee-oodad
for the town hall	**para el ayuntamiento?**
	para el a-yoontam-yento
for St John's church	**para la iglesia de San Juan?**
	para la eegles-ya deh san hwan
for the swimming pool	**para la piscina?**
	para la pis-theena
Is this ...	**¿Es éste ...**
	es esteh ...
the bus for the market place?	**el autobús para el mercado?**
	el ah-ooto-boos para el maircad-o
the tram for the railway station?	**el tranvía para la estación de tren?**
	el trambeea para la estath-yon deh tren
Where can I get a taxi?	**¿Dónde puedo tomar un taxi?**
	dondeh pwed-o tom-ar oon taxi
Can you put me off at the right stop, please?	**¿Puede avisarme en mi parada, por favor?**
	pwed-eh absee-sarmeh en mee parad-ah por fab-or
Can I book a seat?	**¿Puedo reservar un asiento?**
	pwed-o res-airbar oon as-yento

A single	**Un billete de ida solamente** oon bee-yet-eh deh *eeda* solamenteh
A return	**Un billete de ida y vuelta** oon bee-yet-eh deh *eeda* ee bwelta
First class	**Primera clase** prim-*aira* classeh
Second class	**Segunda clase** seg-*oonda* classeh
One adult	**Un adulto** oon ad*oo*lto
Two adults	**Dos adultos** dos ad*oo*ltos
and one child	**y un niño** ee *oon* n*ee*n-yo
and two children	**y dos niños** ee d*o*s n*ee*n-yos
How much is it?	**¿Cuánto es?** cw*a*nto es

LIKELY REACTIONS

Over there	**Allí** ay*ee*
Here	**Aquí** ak-*ee*
Platform (1)	**Andén (primero)** and*e*n (prim-*airo*)
At (four o'clock) [*For times, see p. 133*]	**A las (cuatro)** ah las (cw*a*tro)
Change at (Zaragoza)	**Cambie en (Zaragoza)** camb-yeh en (tharrag*o*tha)
Change at (the town hall)	**Cambie en (el ayuntamiento)** camb-yeh en (el a-yoontam-y*e*nto)
This is your stop	**Esta es su parada** esta es soo parad-ah
There is only first class	**Sólo hay primera clase** solo *ah*-ee prim-*aira* classeh
There is a supplement	**Hay un suplemento** *ah*-ee oon sooplem*e*nto

Leisure

ESSENTIAL INFORMATION

- Finding the way to a place of entertainment, see p. 17.
- For times of day, see p. 133.
- Important signs, see p. 125.
- It is quite normal for most shows, films or plays, to have a late night session and for the performance to end at 1 or 2 a.m.
- Smoking is strictly forbidden in movies and theatres. You should tip the ushers or usherettes.
- Most movie and theatre seats can be booked in advance.
- In bars, cafés and restaurants it is customary to leave a tip, even if you drink at the counter; and you pay when you leave.

WHAT TO SAY

At what times does . . . open?	¿A qué hora abre . . .
	ah keh ora *ab*-reh . . .
the art gallery	la galería de arte?
	la gal-er*eea* deh *art*-eh
the botanical garden	el jardín botánico?
	el hard*een* bot*anic*-o
the cinema	el cine?
	el th*in*-eh
the concert hall	la sala de conciertos?
	la *sal*-ah deh conth-*yairt*os
the disco	la discoteca?
	la discot*ec*-ah
the museum	el museo?
	el moo-*sey*-o
the nightclub	la sala de fiestas?
	la *sal*-ah deh fee-*est*as
the sports stadium	el estadio de deportes?
	el est*ad*-yo deh dep-*ort*-es
the swimming pool	la piscina?
	la pis-th*eena*
the theatre	el teatro?
	el teh-*atro*
the zoo	el zoo?
	el *thoh*-o

At what time does ... close?	**¿A qué hora cierra ...**
	ah keh *o*ra thee-*e*rra ...
the art gallery	**la galería de arte?**
	la gal-er*ee*a deh *a*rt-eh
[*see above list*]	
At what time does ... start?	**¿A qué hora empieza ...**
	ah keh *o*ra emp-y*e*th-ah ...
the cabaret	**el cabaret?**
	el cabar*e*t
the concert	**el concierto?**
	el conth-y*air*to
the film	**la película?**
	la pel*ee*coo-la
the match	**el partido?**
	el part*ee*do
the play	**la obra?**
	la *o*bra
the race	**la carrera?**
	la carr*air*a
How much is it ...	**¿Cuánto es ...**
	cw*a*nto es ...
for an adult?	**por un adulto?**
	por oon ad*oo*lto
for a child?	**por un niño?**
	por oon n*ee*n-yo
Two adults, please	**Dos adultos, por favor**
	dos ad*oo*ltos por fab-*o*r
Three children, please	**Tres niños, por favor**
	tres n*ee*n-yos por fab-*o*r
[*State price, if there's a choice*]	
Stalls/circle/sun/shade	**Butaca/anfiteatro/sol/sombra**
	boot*a*c-ah/anfee-teh-*a*tro/sol/
	s*o*mbra
Do you have ...	**¿Tiene ...**
	tee-*e*n-eh ...
a programme?	**un programa?**
	oon progr*a*mma
a guide book?	**una guía?**
	*oo*na gh*ee*a
Where's the toilet, please?	**¿Dónde están los servicios, por**
	favor?
	d*o*ndeh est*a*n los sairb*i*th-yos por
	fab-*o*r

Where's the cloakroom?	¿Dónde está el guardarropa?
	dondeh esta el gwarda-ropa
I would like lessons in ...	Quiero lecciones de ...
	kee-*ai*ro lekth-*yon*-es deh ...
skiing	esquí
	esk*ee*
sailing	vela
	b*el*-ah
water skiing	esquí acuático
	esk*ee* aqu*a*tic-o
sub-aqua diving	buceo
	booth*eh*-o
Can I hire ...	¿Puedo alquilar ...
	pw*ed*-o alkeel*ar* ...
some skis?	unos esquís?
	*oo*nos esk*ee*s
some skiboots?	unas botas de esquí?
	*oo*nas bot-as deh esk*ee*
a boat?	un bote?
	oon bot-eh
a fishing rod?	una caña de pescar?
	*oo*na can-ya deh pesc*ar*
a deck-chair?	una hamaca?
	*oo*na am*a*cca
a sun umbrella?	una sombrilla?
	*oo*na sombr*ee*-ya
the necessary equipment?	el equipo necesario?
	el ek*ee*po nethes*arr*io
How much is it ...	¿Cuánto es ...
	cw*anto* es ...
per day/per hour?	por día/por hora?
	por d*ee*a/por *o*ra
Do I need a licence?	¿Necesito licencia?
	neth-es*ee*to leethenth-*ya*

Asking if things are allowed

ESSENTIAL INFORMATION

- May one smoke here?
  May we smoke here?
  May I smoke here?
  Can one smoke here?
  Can we smoke here?
  Can I smoke here?

  ¿Se puede fumar aquí?

- All these English variations can be expressed in one way in Spanish. To save space, only the first English version (May one . . . ?) is shown below.

WHAT TO SAY

Excuse me, please	**Perdone, por favor** pairdon-eh por fab-*or*
May one . . .	**¿Se puede . . .** seh pw*ed*-eh . . .
camp here?	**acampar aquí?** acamp*ar* ak-*ee*
come in?	**entrar?** entr*ar*
dance here?	**bailar aquí?** by-l*ar* ak-*ee*
fish here?	**pescar aquí?** pesc*ar* ak-*ee*
get a drink here?	**obtener una bebida aquí?** obten-*air* *oo*na bebeeda ak-*ee*
get out this way?	**salir por aquí?** saleer por ak-*ee*
get something to eat here?	**obtener algo de comer?** obten-*air* *a*lgo deh com-*air*
leave one's things here?	**dejar las cosas aquí?** deh-h*ar* las c*os*-as ak-*ee*
look around?	**mirar esto?** mee-r*ar* *e*sto
park here?	**aparcar aquí?** aparc*ar* ak-*ee*

May one ...	¿Se puede ...
	seh pwed-eh ...
picnic here?	**comer aquí?**
	com-*air* ak-*ee*
sit here?	**sentar aquí?**
	sent*ar* ak-*ee*
smoke here?	**fumar aquí?**
	foom*ar* ak-*ee*
swim here?	**nadar aquí?**
	nad-*ar* ak-*ee*
take photos here?	**tomar fotos aquí?**
	tom-*ar* f*o*tos ak-*ee*
telephone here?	**telefonear aquí?**
	telefoneh-*ar* ak-*ee*
wait here?	**esperar aquí?**
	esper*ar* ak-*ee*

LIKELY REACTIONS

Yes, certainly	**Sí, desde luego**
	s*ee* d*e*sdeh lw*e*g-o
Help yourself	**Sírvase usted mismo**
	s*ee*rba-seh oosted m*i*smo
I think so	**Creo que sí**
	creh-o keh s*ee*
Of course	**Claro**
	cl*a*r-o
Yes, but be careful	**Sí, pero tenga cuidado**
	s*ee* p*e*rro tenga cweed*a*d-o
No, certainly not	**No, desde luego que no**
	n*o* d*e*sdeh lw*e*g-o keh n*o*
I don't think so	**No creo**
	no creh-o
Not normally	**Normalmente no**
	norm*a*lmenteh no
Sorry	**Lo siento**
	lo see-*e*nto

Reference

PUBLIC NOTICES

- Key words on signs for drivers, pedestrians, travellers, shoppers and overnight guests.

ABIERTO	Open
ADUANA	Customs
AGUA POTABLE	Drinking water
ALQUILER DE COCHES	Cars for rent
ALTO	Halt
ANDEN	Platform
APARCAMIENTO	Car park
ASCENSOR	Lift
ASEOS	Toilets
ATENCION AL TREN	Beware of the trains
AUTOBUS SOLAMENTE	For buses (only)
AUTOPISTA	Highway
AUTOSERVICIO	Self-service
BADEN PERMANENTE	In constant use (no parking)
BAR	Bar
BAÑOS	Baths
CABALLEROS	Gentlemen
CAJA	Cash desk
CALIENTE	Hot (tap)
CALZADA DETERIORADA	Bad surface
CALLEJON SIN SALIDA	Dead end
CAMINO CERRADO	Road closed
CAÑADA	Cattle crossing
CAZA	Hunting
CEDA EL PASO	Yield
CENTRO CIUDAD	Town centre
CERRADO	Closed
CERRADO POR VACACIONES	Closed for holiday period
CIRCULACION EN AMBAS DIRECCIONES	Two-way traffic
CIRCULEN POR LA DERECHA	Keep right

COCHE-RESTAURANTE	Dining car
COMEDOR	Dining room
COMPLETO	No vacancies
CONSERJE	Porter
CONSIGNA	Left luggage
CRUCE	Crossroads
CRUCE DE CICLISTAS	Bike crossing
CRUCE DE BAÑO	Bathroom
CUIDADO	Watch out
CUIDADO CON EL PERRO	Beware of the dog
CURVA PELIGROSA	Dangerous curve
DAMAS	Ladies
DESPACIO	Drive slowly
DESPACHO DE BILLETES	Ticket office
DESPRENDIMIENTO DEL TERRENO	Falling stones
DESVIO	Detour
DIRECCION UNICA	One-way (street)
DISCO OBLIGATORIO	Parking tokens required
DUCHA	Shower
EMPUJE	Push
ENCIENDA LOS FAROS	Lights on
ENTRADA	Entrance
ENTRADA LIBRE	Admission/Entrance free
ENTRE SIN LLAMAR	Enter without knocking
ES PELIGROSO ASOMARSE AL EXTERIOR	It's dangerous to lean out of the window
ESCALERA AUTOMATICA	Escalator
ESCUELA	School
ESPERE	Wait
ESTACIONAMIENTO LIMITADO	Resricted parking
ESTRECHAMIENTO DE CALZADA	Road narrows
FINAL DE AUTOPISTA	End (highway)
FIRME (SUPERFICIE) DESLIZANTE	Slippery surface (road)
FRIO	Cold
GUIA	Guide
HORAS DE VISITA	Visiting hours

INFORMACION	Information office/desk
JORNADA INTENSIVA	Shop opens early in the morning and closes in the afternoon (e.g. 8 a.m. – 2 p.m.)
LAVABOS	Lavatories
LIQUIDACION	Sale
LLAME A LA PUERTA	Knock (door)
LLAME AL TIMBRE	Ring (bell)
LLEGADAS	Arrivals
MAYORES	Adults
METRO	Underground (train)
NIÑOS	Children
NO HAY ENTRADAS (LOCALIDADES)	House full (movie, theatre etc)
NO POTABLE	Not for drinking
NO SE ADMITEN CARAVANAS	No caravans
NO TOCAR	Do not touch
OBJETOS PERDIDOS	Lost property
OBRAS	Construction
OCUPADO	Occupied
OFERTA ESPECIAL	Special offer
OJO AL TREN	Beware of the trains
PARADA	Stop
PASEN	Cross (the road)
PASO A NIVEL	Level crossing
PASO SUBTERRANEO	Subway
PEAJE	Toll
PEATON, CIRCULA POR TU IZQUIERDA	Pedestrian keep to the left
PEATONES	Pedestrians
PELIGRO	Danger
PELIGRO DE INCENDIO	Danger of fire
PESCA	Fishing
PISO (PRIMERO, SEGUNDO, TERCERO, PLANTA BAJA SOTANO	Floor (first, second, third, ground, basement)
PLAZAS LIBRES	Vacancies
POLICIA	Police
PRECAUCION	Caution
PRECIOS FIJOS	Fixed prices

PRINCIPIO DE AUTOPISTA	Start (of highway)
PRIORIDAD A LA DERECHA	Priority to the right
PRIVADO	Private
PROHIBIDO	Forbidden
PROHIBIDO ADELANTAR	Passing forbidden
PROHIBIDO APARCAR	No parking
PROHIBIDO BAÑARSE SIN GORRO	No bathing without a cap
PROHIBIDO EL PASO	Trespassers will be prosecuted
PROHIBIDO FUMAR	No smoking
PROHIBIDO HABLAR AL CONDUCTOR	No talking to the driver
PROHIBIDO HACER CAMPING	No camping
PROHIBIDO PISAR EL CESPED	Keep off the grass
PROHIBIDO TOMAR FOTOGRAFIAS	No photographs
REBAJAS	Sales
RECIEN PINTADO	Wet paint
RECEPCION	Reception
REDUZCA VELOCIDAD	Slow down
RESERVADO	Reserved
RESERVAS	Reservations
RETRETE	Toilets
SALA DE ESPERA	Waiting room
SALDOS	Sales
SALIDA	Exit
SALIDA DE EMERGENCIA	Emergency exit
SALIDAS	Departures
SE ALQUILA HABITACION	Room for rent
SE PROHIBE LA ENTRADA	No admission/no entry
SE VENDE	For sale
SEMAFORO	Traffic lights
SEÑORAS	Ladies
SEÑORES	Gentlemen
SERVICIOS	Toilets
SIGA ADELANTE	Go

SILENCIO	Quiet
TAQUILLA	Ticket office
VEHICULOS PESADOS	For heavy vehicles
VELOCIDAD LIMITADA	Speed limit
VENENO	Poison
VENTA	For sale
VENTANILLA	Window (of booking office)
ZONA AZUL	Restricted parking
ZONA DE AVALANCHAS	Avalanche area

ABBREVIATIONS

A	Albergue	inn/hostel
ANCE	Agrupación Nacional de campings de España	Spanish Federation of Camping Sites
apdo	apartado (de correos)	post office box
Av/Avda	Avenida	avenue
C	Carretera comarcal	provincial road
	Caliente	hot (water tap)
C/	Calle	street
	Cuenta	account
CAMPSA	Compañía Arrendataria del Monopolio de petróleos Sociedad Anónima	National petrol company
cént(s)	céntimo(s)	hundredth part of a peseta
CN	Carretera Nacional	national road
CT	Centro Turístico	tourist centre
CTNE	Compañia Telefónica Nacional de España	Spanish Telephone company
dcha	derecha	right
do	descuento	discount
F	Frío	cold (water tap)
FC	Ferrocarril	railway
FEVE	Ferrocarriles Españoles de Via Estrecha	Spanish railway company
GC	Guardia Civil	Civil Guard
h	hora	hour
	habitantes	inhabitants
	hacia	circa
IB	Iberia	Spanish aviation company

izq	izquierdo	left
km/h	kilómetros por hora	kilometres per hour
kv	kilovatios	kilowatts
L	Carretera Local	local road
	Libra	English pound
Lleg	Llegadas	Arrivals
MIT	Ministerio de Información y Turismo	Ministry of Tourism
N	Nacional (carretera)	national road
	norte	north
nº] num.	número	number
NO	noroeste	northwest
OP	Obras Públicas	Public Works
Pº	Paseo	avenue
pta(s)	peseta(s)	peseta(s)
PVP	Precio de Venta al Público	Sale price to the public
RACE	Real Automóvil Club de España	Royal Automobile Club of Spain
REAJ	Red Española de Albergues Juveniles	Youth Hostel Association
RENFE	Red Nacional de Ferrocarriles Españoles	Spanish national railway company
Sal	Salidas	Departures
Sr	Señor	Mr
Sra	Señora	Mrs
Sres	Señores	Messrs
Srta	Señorita	Miss
SP	Servicio Público	Public Service (taxis and buses)
SR	Sin Reserva	without reservation
Tfno	Teléfono	Telephone
TVE	Televisión Española	Spanish television company
Vda de	viuda de	widow of
vg, vgr	verbigracia	namely

NUMBERS

Cardinal numbers

0	cero	th*ai*ro
1	uno	*oo*no
2	dos	d*o*s
3	tres	tr*e*s
4	cuatro	cw*a*tro
5	cinco	th*i*nko
6	seis	s*ey*s
7	siete	see-*e*t-eh
8	ocho	*o*cho
9	nueve	nw*e*b-eh
10	diez	dee-*e*th
11	once	*o*ntheh
12	doce	d*o*th-eh
13	trece	tr*e*th-eh
14	catorce	cat-*o*rtheh
15	quince	k*i*ntheh
16	dieciséis	dee-ethee-s*ey*s
17	diecisiete	dee-ethee-see-*e*t-eh
18	dieciocho	dee-ethee-*o*cho
19	diecinueve	dee-ethee-nw*e*b-eh
20	veinte	b*ey*nteh
21	veintiuno	beyntee-*oo*no
22	veintidós	beyntee-d*o*s
23	veintitrés	beyntee-tr*e*s
24	veinticuatro	beyntee-cw*a*tro
25	veinticinco	beyntee-th*i*nko
26	veintiséis	beyntee-s*ey*s
27	veintisiete	beyntee-see-*e*t-eh
28	veintiocho	beyntee-*o*cho
29	veintinueve	beyntee-nw*e*b-eh
30	treinta	tr*ey*nta
31	treinta y uno	tr*ey*nta ee *oo*no
35	treinta y cinco	tr*ey*nta ee th*i*nko
38	treinta y ocho	tr*ey*nta ee *o*cho
40	cuarenta	cwa-r*e*nta
41	cuarenta y uno	cwa-r*e*nta ee *oo*no
45	cuarenta y cinco	cwa-r*e*nta ee th*i*nko
48	cuarenta y ocho	cwa-r*e*nta ee *o*cho

50	cincuenta	thin-cwenta
55	cincuenta y cinco	thin-cwenta ee thinko
60	sesenta	ses-enta
65	sesenta y cinco	ses-enta ee thinko
70	setenta	set-enta
75	setenta y cinco	set-enta ee thinko
80	ochenta	ochenta
85	ochenta y cinco	ochenta ee thinko
90	noventa	nobenta
95	noventa y cinco	nobenta ee thinko
100	cien	thee-en
101	ciento uno	thee-ento oono
102	ciento dos	thee-ento dos
125	ciento veinticinco	thee-ento beyntee-thinko
150	ciento cincuenta	thee-ento thin-cwenta
175	ciento setenta y cinco	thee-ento set-enta ee thinko
200	doscientos	dos-thee-entos
300	trescientos	tres-thee-entos
400	cuatrocientos	cwatro-thee-entos
500	quinientos	kin-yentos
1000	mil	mil
1500	mil quinientos	mil kin-yentos
2000	dos mil	dos mil
5000	cinco mil	thinko mil
10,000	diez mil	dee-eth mil
100,000	cien mil	thee-en mil
1,000,000	un millón	oon mil-yon

Ordinal numbers

1st	primero (1°)	prim-airo
2nd	segundo (2°)	se-goondo
3rd	tercero (3°)	tair-thairo
4th	cuarto (4°)	cwarto
5th	quinto (5°)	kinto
6th	sexto (6°)	sexto
7th	séptimo (7°)	septeemo
8th	octavo (8°)	octabo-o
9th	noveno (9°)	nob-en-o
10th	décimo (10°)	deth-eemo
11th	undécimo onceno	undeth-eemo onth-eno
12th	duodécimo	doo-odeth-eemo

TIME

What time is it?	**¿Qué hora es?**
	keh *ora* es
It's one o'clock	**Es la una**
	es la *oo*na
It's ...	**Son ...**
	son ...
two o'clock	las dos
	las dos
three o'clock	las tres
	las tres
four o'clock	**las cuatro**
	las *cw*atro
in the morning	**de la mañana**
	deh la man-*yanna*
in the afternoon ⎤	**de la tarde**
in the evening ⎦	deh la *tardeh*
at night	**de la noche**
	deh la *noch*-eh
It's ...	**Es ...**
	es ...
noon	mediodía
	med-yo-*deea*
midnight	medianoche
	med-ya-*noch*-eh
It's ...	**Son ...**
	son ...
five past five	**las cinco y cinco**
	las *think*o ee *think*o
ten past five	**las cinco y diez**
	las *think*o ee dee-*eth*
a quarter past five	**las cinco y cuarto**
	las *think*o ee *cw*arto
twenty past five	**las cinco y veinte**
	las *think*o ee *beynteh*
twenty-five past five	**las cinco y veinticinco**
	las *think*o ee beyntee-*think*o
half past five	**las cinco y media**
	las *think*o ee med-ya
twenty-five to six	**las seis menos veinticinco**
	las *seys* men-os beyntee-*think*o

twenty to six	**las seis menos veinte** las seys men-os beynteh
quarter to six	**las seis menos cuarto** las seys men-os cwarto
ten to six	**las seis menos diez** las seys men-os dee-eth
five to six	**las seis menos cinco** las seys men-os thinko
At what time (does the train leave)?	**¿A qué hora (sale el tren)?** ah keh ora (sal-eh el tren)
At ...	**A las ...** ah las ...
13.00	**trece** treth-eh
14.05	**catorce cero cinco** cat-ortheh thairo thinko
15.10	**quinze diez** kin-theh dee-eth
16.15	**dieciséis quince** dee-ethee-seys kintheh
17.20	**diecisiete veinte** dee-ethee-see-et-eh beynteh
18.25	**dieciocho veinticinco** dee-ethee-ocho beynteh-thinko
19.30	**diecinueve treinte** dee-ethee-nweb-eh treynta
20.35	**veinte treinta y cinco** beynteh treynta ee thinko
21.40	**veintiuna cuarenta** beyntee-oona cwa-renta
22.45	**veintidós cuarenta y cinco** beyntee-dos cwa-renta ee thinko
23.50	**veintitrés cincuenta** beyntee-tres thin-cwenta
0.55	**cero cincuenta y cinco** thairo thin-cwenta ee thinko
in ten minutes	**en diez minutos** en dee-eth minootos
in a quarter of an hour	**en un cuarto de ora** en oon cwarto deh ora
in half an hour	**en media hora** en med-ya ora
in three quarters of an hour	**en tres cuartos de hora** en tres cwartos deh ora

DAYS

Monday	**lunes**
	loon-es
Tuesday	**martes**
	mart-es
Wednesday	**miércoles**
	mee-aircol-es
Thursday	**jueves**
	hweb-es
Friday	**viernes**
	bee-airn-es
Saturday	**sábado**
	sabad-o
Sunday	**domingo**
	domingo
last Monday	**el lunes pasado**
	el loon-es pasad-o
next Tuesday	**el martes próximo**
	el mart-es proxim-o
on Wednesday	**el miércoles**
	el mee-aircol-es
on Thursdays	**los jueves**
	los hweb-es
until Friday	**hasta el viernes**
	asta el bee-airn-es
before Saturday	**antes del sábado**
	ant-es del sabad-o
after Sunday	**después del domingo**
	despwes del domingo
the day before yesterday	**anteayer**
	anteh-ayair
two days ago	**hace dos días**
	ath-eh dos dee-as
yesterday	**ayer**
	ayair
yesterday morning	**ayer por la mañana**
	ayair por la man-yanna
yesterday afternoon	**ayer por la tarde**
	ayair por la tardeh
last night	**la noche pasada**
	la noch-eh pasad-ah
today	**hoy**
	oy

this morning	esta mañana
	esta man-yanna
this afternoon	esta tarde
	esta tardeh
tonight	esta noche
	esta noch-eh
tomorrow	mañana
tomorrow morning]	man-yanna
tomorrow afternoon	mañana por la mañana
	manyan-a por la man-yanna
tomorrow evening	mañana por la tarde
	man-yanna por la tardeh
tomorrow night	mañana por la noche
	man-yanna por la noch-eh
the day after tomorrow	pasado mañana
	pasad-o man-yanna

MONTHS AND DATES

January	enero
	en-airo
February	febrero
	feb-rairo
March	marzo
	martho
April	abril
	abril
May	mayo
	ma-yo
June	junio
	hoon-yo
July	julio
	hool-yo
August	agosto
	a-gosto
September	septiembre
	sept-yembreh
October	octubre
	octoobreh
November	noviembre
	nob-yembreh
December	diciembre
	dith-yembreh

in January	**en enero**
	en en-*airo*
until February	**hasta febrero**
	*a*sta feb-*rairo*
before March	**antes de marzo**
	*a*nt-es deh m*a*rtho
after April	**después de abril**
	despw*e*s deh abr*i*l
during May	**durante mayo**
	doo-r*a*nteh m*a*-yo
not until June	**hasta junio no**
	*a*sta h*o*on-yo no
the beginning of July	**principios de julio**
	pr*i*nth*i*p-yos deh h*o*ol-yo
the middle of August	**mediados de agosto**
	med-y*a*d-os deh ag*o*sto
the end of September	**finales de septiembre**
	fin-*a*l-es deh sept-y*e*mbreh
last month	**el mes pasado**
	el m*e*s pas*a*do
this month	**este mes**
	*e*steh m*e*s
next month	**el mes próximo**
	el m*e*s pr*o*xim-o
in spring	**en primavera**
	en preema-b*aira*
in summer	**en verano**
	en beh-r*a*n-o
in autumn	**en otoño**
	en ot*o*n-yo
in winter	**en invierno**
	en imb-y*airno*
this year	**este año**
	*e*steh *a*n-yo
last year	**el año pasado**
	el *a*n-yo pas*a*d-o
next year	**el año próximo**
	el *a*n-yo pr*o*xim-o
in 1982	**en mil novecientos ochenta y dos**
	en m*i*l nobeh-th*e*e-*e*ntos och*e*nta ee d*o*s
in 1985	**en mil novecientos ochenta y cinco**
	en m*i*l nobeh-th*e*e-*e*ntos och*e*nta ee th*i*nko

in 1990	**en mil novecientos noventa**
	en mil nobeh-thee-entos nobenta
What's the date today?	**¿Qué fecha es hoy?**
	keh fech-ah es oy
It's the 6th of March	**Es el seis de marzo**
	es el seys deh martho
It's the 12th of April	**Es el doce de abril**
	es el doth-eh deh abril
It's the 21st of August	**Es el veintiuno de agosto**
	es el beyntee-oono deh agosto

Public holidays

● On these days, offices, shops and schools are closed.

1 January	**Año Nuevo**	New Year's Day
6 January	**Epifania**	Epiphany
	Día de Reyes]	
19 March	**San José**	St Joseph's Day
...	**Jueves Santo**	Maundy Thursday
...	**Viernes Santo**	Good Friday
...	**Día de la Ascensión**	Ascension Thursday
	Corpus Christi	Corpus Christi Day
1 May	**Día del Trabajo**	Labour Day
25 July	**San Jaime**]	St James's Day
	Día de Santiago]	
15 August	**Día de la Asuncion**	Assumption Day
12 October	**Día del Pilar** ┐	Columbus Day
	Fiesta de la Hispanidad ┘	
1 November	**Todos los Santos**	All Saints Day
8 December	**Inmaculada Concepción**	Immaculate Conception Day
25 December	**Navidad**	Christmas Day

COUNTRIES AND NATIONALITIES

Countries

Australia	**Australia**
	owstral-ya
Austria	**Austria**
	owstr-ia
Belgium	**Bélgica**
	bel-heeca
Britain	**Gran Bretaña**
	gran bret-an-ya

Canada	**Canadá** canad*a*
East Africa	**Africa del Este** *a*frica del esteh
Eire	**Eire** *a*ireh
England	**Inglaterra** ingla-te*rra*
France	**Francia** fr*a*nth-ya
Greece	**Grecia** greth-ya
India	**India** *i*ndia
Italy	**Italia** ital-ya
Luxembourg	**Luxemburgo** looxemb*o*org-o
Netherlands	**Los Paises Bajos** los pa-*ees*-es b*a*-hos
New Zealand	**Nueva Zelanda** nw*e*b-ah thel-*a*nda
Northern Ireland	**Irlanda del Norte** eer-l*a*nda del n*o*rteh
Pakistan	**Pakistán** pakist*a*n
Portugal	**Portugal** portoog*a*l
Scotland	**Escocia** escoth-ya
South Africa	**Sudáfrica** sood-*a*frica
Spain	**España** esp*a*n-**ya**
Switzerland	**Suiza** sw*ee*tha
United States	**Estados Unidos** est*a*d-os oon*ee*dos
Wales	**Gales** g*a*l-es
West Germany	**Alemania occidental** al-emm*a*n-ya ok-theeden-t*a*l
West Indies	**Antillas** ant*ee*-yas

Nationalities

American	**americano/americana**
	americano/americana
Australian	**australiano/australiana**
	owstral-yan-o/owstral-yan-ah
British	**británico/británica**
	britan-ico/britan-ica
Canadian	**Canadiense**
	canad-yen-seh
East African	**africano/africana del este**
	africano/ africana del esteh
English	**inglés/inglesa**
	in-gles/in-gles-ah
Indian	**Hindú**
	in-doo
Irish	**irlandés/irlandesa**
	eerland-es/eerland-es-ah
a New Zealander	**neozelandés/neozelandesa**
	neo-thel-and-es/neo-thel-and-es-ah
a Pakistani	**pakistaní**
	pakistanee
Scots	**escocés/escocesa**
	escoth-es/escoth-es-ah
South African	**sudafricano/sudafricana**
	sood-africano/sood-africana
Welsh	**galés/galesa**
	gal-es/gal-es-ah
West Indian	**antillano/antillana**
	anti-yan-o/anti-yan-ah

DEPARTMENT STORE GUIDE

Alfombras	Carpets
Alimentación	Food
Artículos de deporte	Sports
Artículos de limpieza	Cleaning materials
Artículos de montaña	Mountaineering department
Artículos de piel	Leather goods
Artículos de playa	Beach accessories
Artículos de viaje	Travel articles
Baterías de cocina	Kitchen utensils
Blusas	Blouses
Bolsos	Bags
Bricolage	Do it yourself
Caballeros	Menswear
Cafetería	Café
Caja	Checkout
Camisas	Shirts
Camisería	Shirt department
Camping	Camping
Cinturones	Belts
Cojines	Cushions
Confecciones	Ready-made clothing
Corbatas	Ties
Cortinas	Curtains
Cosméticos	Cosmetics
Cristalería	Glassware
Cuarto/Cuarta	Fourth
Cubiertas	Coverlets
Discos	Records
Droguería	Toiletries
Electrodomésticos	Electric appliances
Fajas	Girdles
Ferretería	Hardware
Fotografía	Photography
Guantes	Gloves
Hogar	Home furnishing
Información	Information
Jardinería	Garden
Jerseys	Pullovers
Joyería	Jewellery
Juguetes	Toys
Laminados	Laminates
Lencería	Lingerie

Librería	Books
Loza	Earthenware
Mantas	Blankets
Mantelerías	Table linen
Medias	Stockings
Mercería	Haberdashery
Moda juvenil	Young fashion
Modas señora	Ladies fashions
Muebles	Furniture
Muebles de cocina	Kitchen furniture
Niños/Niñas	Children
Oportunidades	Special offers
Pañería	Drapery
Papelería	Stationery
Perfumería	Perfumery
Piso	Floor
Planta	Floor
Planta baja	Ground floor
Porcelana	China
Primero	First
Radio	Radio
Reclamaciones	Complaints
Regalos	Gifts
Relojería	Watches
Retales	Materials
Ropa confeccionada	Ready-made clothing
Ropa de cama	Bedding
Ropa infantil	Children's wear
Ropa interior	Underwear
Sección	Department
Segundo	Second
Señora/Señoras	Ladies' Wear
Sombrerería	Millinery
Sostenes	Bras
Sótano	Basement
Sujetadores	Bras
Tapicerias	Furnishing fabrics
Televisión	Television
Tercero	Third
Vajilla	Crockery
Ventas a crédito	Accounts
Zapatería	Footwear
Zapatillas	Slippers

CONVERSION TABLES

Read the centre column of these tables from right to left to convert from metric to imperial and from left to right to convert from imperial to metric e.g. 5 litres = 8.80 pints; 5 pints = 2.84 litres.

pints		litres		gallons		litres
1.76	1	0.57		0.22	1	4.55
3.52	2	1.14		0.44	2	9.09
5.28	3	1.70		0.66	3	13.64
7.07	4	2.27		0.88	4	18.18
8.80	5	2.84		1.00	5	22.73
10.56	6	3.41		1.32	6	27.28
12.32	7	3.98		1.54	7	31.82
14.08	8	4.55		1.76	8	36.37
15.84	9	5.11		1.98	9	40.91

ounces		grams		pounds		kilos
0.04	1	28.35		2.20	1	0.45
0.07	2	56.70		4.41	2	0.91
0.11	3	85.05		6.61	3	1.36
0.14	4	113.40		8.82	4	1.81
0.18	5	141.75		11.02	5	2.27
0.21	6	170.10		13.23	6	2.72
0.25	7	198.45		15.43	7	3.18
0.28	8	226.80		17.64	8	3.63
0.32	9	255.15		19.84	9	4.08

inches		centimetres		yards		metres
0.39	1	2.54		1.09	1	0.91
0.79	2	5.08		2.19	2	1.83
1.18	3	7.62		3.28	3	2.74
1.58	4	10.16		4.37	4	3.66
1.95	5	12.70		5.47	5	4.57
2.36	6	15.24		6.56	6	5.49
2.76	7	17.78		7.66	7	6.40
3.15	8	20.32		8.65	8	7.32
3.54	9	22.86		9.84	9	8.23

miles		kilometres
0.62	1	1.61
1.24	2	3.22
1.86	3	4.83
2.49	4	6.44
3.11	5	8.05
3.73	6	9.66
4.35	7	11.27
4.97	8	12.87
5.59	9	14.48

A quick way to convert kilometres to miles: divide by 8 and multiply by 5. To convert miles to kilometres: divide by 5 and multiply by 8.

fahrenheit (°F)	centigrade (°C)		lbs/ sq in	k/ sq cm
212°	100° boiling point		18	1.3
100°	38°		20	1.4
98.4°	36.9° body temperature		22	1.5
86°	30°		25	1.7
77°	25°		29	2.0
68°	20°		32	2.3
59°	15°		35	2.5
50°	10°		36	2.5
41°	5°		39	2.7
32°	0° freezing point		40	2.8
14°	−10°		43	3.0
−4°	−20°		45	3.2
			46	3.2
			50	3.5
			60	4.2

To convert °C to °F: divide by 5, multiply by 9 and add 32. To convert °F to °C: take away 32, divide by 9 and multiply by 5.

CLOTHING SIZES

Remember – always try on clothes before buying. Clothing sizes are usually unreliable.

women's dresses and suits

Europe	38	40	42	44	46	48
UK	32	34	36	38	40	42
USA	10	12	14	16	18	20

men's suits and coats

Europe	46	48	50	52	54	56
UK and USA	36	38	40	42	44	46

men's shirts

Europe	36	37	38	39	41	42	43
UK and USA	14	14½	15	15½	16	16½	17

socks

Europe	38–39	39–40	40–41	41–42	42–43
UK and USA	9½	10	10½	11	11½

shoes

Europe	34	35½	36½	38	39	41	42	43	44	45
UK	2	3	4	5	6	7	8	9	10	11
USA	3½	4½	5½	6½	7½	8½	9½	10½	11½	12½

Do it yourself

Some notes on the language

This section does not deal with 'grammar' as such. The purpose here is to explain some of the most obvious and elementary nuts and bolts of the language, based on the principal phrases included in the book. This information should enable you to produce numerous sentences of your own making.

There is no pronunciation guide in this section, partly because it would get in the way of the explanations and partly because you have to do it yourself at this stage if you are serious – work out the pronunciation from all the earlier examples in the book.

THE

All nouns in Spanish belong to one of two genders: masculine or feminine, irrespective of whether they refer to living beings or inanimate objects.

The (singular)	masculine	feminine
the address		la dirección
the apple		la manzana
the bill		la cuenta
the cup of tea		la taza de té
the glass of wine	el vaso de vino	
the key		la llave
the luggage	el equipaje	
the menu	el menú	
the newspaper	el periódico	
the receipt	el recibo	
the sandwich	el bocadillo	
the suitcase		la maleta
the telephone directory		la guía telefónica
the timetable	el horario	

Important things to remember

- *The* is **el** before a masculine noun and **la** before a feminine noun.
- You can often tell if a singular noun is masculine or feminine by its ending. Masculine nouns usually end in 'o' and feminine nouns in 'a'. However there are several exceptions notably a whole group of nouns which end in 'e' e.g. **el equipaje**, so you should try to learn and remember all genders. If you are reading a word with **el** or **la** in front of it, you can detect its gender immediately: **el menú** is masculine (*m.* in dictionaries) and **la dirección** is feminine (*f.* in dictionaries).
- Does it matter? Not unless you want to make a serious attempt to speak correctly and scratch beneath the surface of the language. You would be understood if you said **la menú** or even **el dirección**, providing your pronunciation was good.

The (plural)	masculine	feminine
the addresses		**las direcciones**
the apples		**las manzanas**
the bills		**las cuentas**
the cups of tea		**las tazas de té**
the glasses of wine	**los vasos de vino**	
the keys		**las llaves**
the luggage (this is only singular in Spanish, see above)		
the menus	**los menús**	
the newspapers	**los periódicos**	
the receipts	**los recibos**	
the sandwiches	**los bocadillos**	
the suitcases		**las maletas**
the telephone directories		**las guías telefónicas**
the timetables	**los horarios**	

Important things to remember

- As a general rule, a noun adds an 's' to become plural. However, a noun ending in a consonant adds 'es' e.g. **la dirección**, **las direcciones**.
- *The* is **los** before masculine nouns in the plural.
- *The* is **las** before feminine nouns in the plural.

Practise saying and writing these sentences in Spanish:

Have you got the key?	**Tiene usted la llave?**
Have you got the luggage?	**Tiene usted . . . ?**
Have you got the telephone directory?	
Have you got the menu?	
I'd like the key	**Quiero la llave**
I'd like the receipt	**Quiero . . .**
I'd like the bill	
I'd like the keys	
Where is the key?	**¿Dónde está la llave**
Where is the timetable?	**¿Dónde está . . . ?**
Where is the address?	
Where is the suitcase?	
Where is the luggage?	
Where are the keys?	**¿Dónde están las llaves?**
Where are the sandwiches?	**¿Dónde están . . . ?**
Where are the apples?	
Where are the suitcases?	
Where can I get the key?	**¿Dónde puedo obtener la llave?**
Where can I get the address?	**¿Dónde puedo obtener . . . ?**
Where can I get the timetables?	

Now make up more sentences along the same lines.
Try adding please: **por favor**, at the end.

A/AN

A/an (singular)	masculine	feminine
an address		**una dirección**
an apple		**una manzana**
a bill		**una cuenta**
a cup of tea		**una taza de té**
a glass of beer	**un vaso de vino**	
a key		**una llave**
a menu	**un menú**	
a newspaper	**un periódico**	
a sandwich	**un bocadillo**	
a suitcase		**una maleta**
a telephone directory		**una guía telefónica**
a timetable	**un horario**	

Some/any (plural)	masculine	feminine
addresses		unas direcciones
apples		unas manzanas
bills		unas cuentas
cups of tea		unas tazas de té
glasses of wine	unos vasos de vino	
keys		unas llaves
luggage	unos equipajes	
menus	unos menús	
newspapers	unos periódicos	
receipts	unos recibos	
sandwiches	unos bocadillos	
suitcases		unas maletas
telephone directories		unas guías telefónicas
timetables	unos horarios	

Important things to remember

- *A* or *an* is **un** before masculine nouns and **una** before feminine nouns.
- The plural, *some* or *any* is **unos** before masculine nouns and **unas** before feminine nouns.
- In certain Spanish expressions, **unos** and **unas** are left out:

See an example of this in the sentences marked * below.

Practise saying and writing these sentences in Spanish:

Have you got a receipt?	¿Tiene usted ... ?
Have you got a menu?	
I'd like a telephone directory	Quiero ...
I'd like some sandwiches	
Where can I get some newspapers?	¿Dónde puedo obtener.... ?
Where can I get a cup of tea?	
Is there a key?	¿Hay una llave?
Is there a timetable?	¿Hay ... ?
Is there a telephone directory?	

Is there a menu?
Are there any keys?   ¿Hay unas llaves?
Are there any newspapers?   ¿Hay ... ?
Are there any sandwiches?

Now make up more sentences along the same lines.
Then try these new phrases:
Tomo ... (I'll have ...)
Necesito ... (I need ...)

I'll have a glass of wine   **Tomo un vaso de vino**
I'll have some sandwiches   **Tomo ...**
I'll have some apples
I need a cup of tea   **Necesito una taza de té**
I need a key   **Necesito ...**
* I need some keys   **Necesito llaves**
* I need some addresses   **Necesito ...**
* I need some sandwiches
* I need some suitcases

SOME/ANY

In cases where *some* or *any* refer to more than one thing, such as
some/any ice-creams and *some/any apples,* unos and unas are
used as explained earlier:
unos helados (some/any ice-creams)
unas manzanas (some/any apples)
As a guide, you can usually *count* the number of containers or
whole items.

In cases where *some* refers to part of a whole thing or an
indefinite quantity in English, there is no Spanish equivalent.
Just leave it out.

Look at the list below:

the beer	la cerveza	some beer	cerveza
the bread	el pan	some bread	pan
the butter	la mantequilla	some butter	mantequilla
the cheese	el queso	some cheese	queso

The same would apply to the following words

the coffee	el café	the sugar	el azúcar
the flour	la harina	the tea	el té
the lemonade	la limonada	the water	el agua
the oil	el aceite	the wine	el vino

Practise saying and writing these sentences in Spanish:

Have you got some coffee?	¿Tiene usted café?
Have you got some flour?	
Have you got some sugar?	
I'd like some butter	Quiero mantequilla
I'd like some oil	
I'd like some bread	
Is there any lemonade?	¿Hay limonada?
Is there any water?	
Is there any wine?	
Where can I get some cheese?	¿Dónde puedo obtener queso?
Where can I get some flour?	
Where can I get some water?	
I'll have some beer	Tomo cerveza
I'll have some tea	
I'll have some coffee	

THIS AND THAT

There are two words in Spanish
   esto (this)
   eso (that)
If you don't know the Spanish for an object, just point and say:

Quiero eso	I'd like that
Tomo esto	I'll have that
Necesito esto	I need this

HELPING OTHERS

You can help yourself with phrases such as:

I'd like . . . a sandwich	Quiero . . . un bocadillo
Where can I get . . . a cup of tea?	¿Donde puedo obtener . . . una taza de té?
I'll have . . . a glass of beer	Tomo . . . un vaso de vino
I need . . . a receipt	Necesito . . . un recibo

If you come across a compatriot having trouble making himself or herself understood, you should be able to speak to the Spanish person on their behalf.

Note that it is not necessary to say the words for *he* (él), *she* (ella) and *I* (yo) in Spanish unless you want to emphasize them e.g. *He'll* have a beer and *I'll* have a glass of wine.

He'd like . . .	(Él) quiere un bocadillo
	(el) kee-*aire*h oon boccad*ee*-yo
She'd like . . .	(Ella) quiere un bocadillo
	el-ya kee-*aire*h oon boccad*ee*-yo
Where can he get . . . ?	¿Dónde puede (él) obtener una taza de té?
	dondeh pwed-eh (el) obten-*air* oona tath-a deh teh
Where can she get . . . ?	¿Dónde puede (ella) obtener una taza de té?
	dondeh pwed-eh (el-ya) obten-*air* oona tath-a deh teh
He'll have . . .	(Él) toma un vaso de vino
	(el) tom-a oon basso deh b*ee*no
She'll have . . .	(Ella) toma un vaso de vino
	(el-ya) tom-a oon basso deh b*ee*no
He needs . . .	(Él) necesita un recibo
	(el) neth-es*ee*ta oon reth*ee*bo
She needs . . .	(Ella) necesita un recibo
	(el-ya) neth-es*ee*ta oon reth*ee*bo

You can also help a couple or a group if they are having difficulties. The Spanish word for *they* is ellos (men) and ellas (women), and ellos (men and women) but it is usually left out altogether. Look at the verb ending:

They'd like . . .	(Ellos) quieren queso
	(el-yos) kee-*aire*n kes-o
They'd like . . .	(Ellas) quieren queso
	(el-yas) kee-*aire*n kes-o

Where can they get ... ?	¿Dónde pueden obtener mantequilla?
	dondeh pwed-en obten-*air* mantehkee-ya
They'll have ...	Toman vino
	tom-an beeno
They need ...	Necesitan agua
	neth-eseetan agwa

What about the two of you? No problem. The word for *we* is nosotros (men) nosotras (women), but it is only really important to change the verb.

We'd like ...	Queremos vino
	keh-rem-os beeno
Where can we get ... ?	¿Dónde podemos obtener agua?
	dondeh pod-em-os obten-*er* agwa
We'll have ...	Tomamos cerveza
	tom-am-os thairbeth-a
We need ...	Necesitamos azúcar
	neth-eseetam-os athoocar

Try writing out your own checklists for these four useful phrase starters, like this:

Quiero ...	Queremos ...
Quiere (él) ...	Quieren (ellos) ...
Quiere (ella) ...	Quieren (ellas) ...
Dónde puedo obtener ... ?	Dónde ... obtener ... ?
Dónde puede (él) obtener ... ?	Dónde ... (ellos) obtener ... ?
Dónde pueden (ellas) obtener ... ?	Dónde ... (ellas) obtener ... ?

MORE PRACTICE

Here are some more Spanish names of things. See how many
different sentences you can make up, using the various points of
information given earlier in this section.

		singular	plural
1	ashtray	cenicero (m)	ceniceros
2	bag	bolsa (f)	bolsas
3	car	coche (m)	coches
4	cigarette	cigarrillo (m)	cigarrillos
5	corkscrew	sacacorchos (m)	sacacorchos
6	garage (repairs)	garaje (m)	garajes
7	grapes	uva (f)	uvas
8	ice-cream	helado (m)	helados
9	knife	cuchillo (m)	cuchillos
10	melon	melón (m)	melones
11	passport	pasaporte (m)	pasaportes
12	postcard	tarjeta postal (f)	tarjetas postales
13	salad	ensalada (f)	ensaladas
14	shoe	zapato (m)	zapatos
15	stamp	sello (m)	sellos
16	station	estación (f)	estaciones
17	street	calle (f)	calles
18	sunglasses		gafas de sol (f)
19	telephone	teléfono (m)	teléfonos
20	ticket	billete (m)	billetes

Index

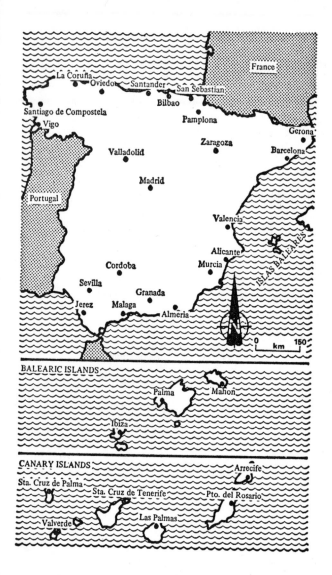

Mexico, Central and South America

FOREIGN LANGUAGE BOOKS

Multilingual
The Insult Dictionary:
 How to Give 'Em Hell in 5 Nasty
 Languages
The Lover's Dictionary:
 How to be Amorous in 5 Delectable
 Languages
Multilingual Phrase Book
Let's Drive Europe Phrasebook
CD-ROM "Languages of the World":
 Multilingual Dictionary Database

Spanish
Vox Spanish and English Dictionaries
The Spanish Businessmate
Nice 'n Easy Spanish Grammar
Spanish Verbs and Essentials of Grammar
Getting Started in Spanish
Spanish à la Cartoon
Guide to Spanish Idioms
Guide to Correspondence in Spanish
The Hispanic Way

French
NTC's New College French and English
 Dictionary
French Verbs and Essentials of Grammar
Getting Started in French
Guide to French Idioms
Guide to Correspondence in French
The French Businessmate
French à la Cartoon
Nice 'n Easy French Grammar
NTC's Dictionary of *Faux Amis*
NTC's Dictionary of Canadian French
Au courant: Expressions for Communicating
 in Everyday French

German
Schöffler-Weis German and English
 Dictionary
Klett German and English Dictionary
Getting Started in German
German Verbs and Essentials of Grammar
Guide to German Idioms
The German Businessmate
Nice 'n Easy German Grammar
German à la Cartoon
NTC's Dictionary of German False Cognates

Italian
Zanichelli New College Italian and English
 Dictionary
Getting Started in Italian
Italian Verbs and Essentials of Grammar

Greek
NTC's New College Greek and English
 Dictionary

Latin
Essentials of Latin Grammar

Hebrew
Everyday Hebrew

Chinese
Easy Chinese Phrasebook and Dictionary

Korean
Korean in Plain English

Swedish
Swedish Verbs and Essentials of Grammar

Russian
Complete Handbook of Russian Verbs
Essentials of Russian Grammar
Business Russian
Basic Structure Practice in Russian

Japanese
Easy Kana Workbook
Easy Hiragana
Easy Katakana
Japanese in Plain English
Everyday Japanese
Japanese for Children
Japanese Cultural Encounters
Nissan's Business Japanese

"Just Enough" Phrase Books
Chinese, Dutch, French, German, Greek,
 Italian, Japanese, Portuguese, Russian,
 Scandinavian, Serbo-Croat, Spanish

Audio and Video Language Programs
Just Listen 'n Learn Spanish, French,
 German, Italian, and Greek
Just Listen 'n Learn...Spanish,
 French, German PLUS
Conversational...Spanish, French, German,
 Italian, Russian, Greek, Japanese, Thai,
 Portuguese in 7 Days
Practice & Improve Your...Spanish,
 French, Italian, and German
Practice & Improve Your...Spanish,
 French, Italian, and German PLUS
VideoPassport French
VideoPassport Spanish
How to Pronounce...Spanish, French,
 German, Italian, Russian, Japanese
 Correctly

PASSPORT BOOKS
a division of *NTC Publishing Group*
4255 West Touhy Avenue
Lincolnwood, Illinois 60646-1975